DICTIONARY
of GESTURES

DICTIONARY of GESTURES

Expressive Comportments and Movements in Use around the World

----

FRANÇOIS CARADEC

ILLUSTRATED BY
PHILIPPE COUSIN

TRANSLATED BY
CHRIS CLARKE

The MIT Press
Cambridge, Massachusetts
London, England

Originally published as *Dictionnaire des gestes: Attitudes et mouvements expressifs en usage dans le monde entier.*
© Librairie Arthème Fayard, 2005.

This book was set in Arnhem Pro and Oxtail by The MIT Press. Printed and bound in the United States of America.

Library of Congress Cataloging-in-Publication Data

Names: Caradec, Francois, author. | Cousin, Philippe, illustrator. | Clarke, Chris (Translator), translator.
Title: Dictionary of gestures : expressive comportments and movements in use around the world / Francois Caradec ; illustrated by Philippe Cousin ; translated by Chris Clarke.
Other titles: Dictionnaire des gestes. English
Description: Cambridge, MA : The MIT Press, [2018] | Translation of: Dictionnaire des gestes : attitudes et mouvements expressifs en usage dans le monde entier. | Includes bibliographical references and index.
Identifiers: LCCN 2018010758 | ISBN 9780262038492 (hardcover : alk. paper)
Subjects: LCSH: Gesture—Dictionaries. | Body language—Dictionaries. | Semiotics—Dictionaries.
Classification: LCC P117 .C2713 2018 | DDC 302.2/22—dc23 LC record available at https://lccn.loc.gov/2018010758

10   9   8   7   6   5   4   3   2   1

In memory of Ivan Lapse

People attach far too much importance to words,
and not nearly enough to the gestures that go with them.
—Boris Vian

CONTENTS

Acknowledgments—ix

ACKNOWLEDGMENTS

To all those who have shown interest in my research over the past thirty years, and in particular, to: François Le Lionnais and Vassilis Alexakis, François Billetdoux, Céline Carlen, Bernard Cerquiglini, Anne F. Garréta, Jean-Paul Goujon, Jacques Jouet, Claude Kannas, Kenji Kitayama, Jacques Legris, Claudia Moatti, Ian Monk, Amélie Remise, Jacques Roubaud, Olivier Salon, François Sullerot.

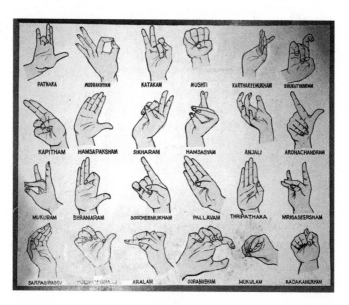

Hand positions used in the Kathakali dance performance in the theater at Ernakulam, Kochi/Cochin of Cochin Cultural Centre (Samgamam, Manikath Road). Photo: Wouter Hagens, public domain.

ON THE BEAUTY
OF GESTURES

CONNECTING GESTURE WITH SPEECH

Because that is the subject of this catalog—it is an inventory of
bodily signs effected *voluntarily* by humankind in order to
communicate with each other.

In this book, all that concerns us are voluntary gestures: I have
avoided as well as I could confounding them with any encoded
expression—of which some examples will nonetheless be found,
belonging to specific codes (the gestures of monks, for instance)
that I felt were picturesque and worthy of being better known;
also included are gestures used in other regions of the world,
which, in comparing them to our own, will allow us to distinguish
numerous "false friends." The "O" formed by the thumb and
index finger in the United States to signify "OK" can also
be a serious insult, most notably in the Arab world, where it is
an obscene gesture.

There are no universal gestures. Thus Western good manners
would have us look at the person with whom we are speaking,
whereas in Asia and Africa we do not look directly at a person
whom we respect—an opposition that can sometimes result in
conflict if a person misreads politeness or deference for disdain
or aggression.

Gestures also change over time, which explains the interest in
studying the gestures made by the orators of antiquity or Europe's
Middle Ages. When the *Rules of Puerile and Respectable Civility*,
published by the Bibliothèque Bleue in Troyes, said that it "isn't

proper to walk with your hands behind your back, it is always the mark of idle folk, they should not be imitated," we can deduce from this that hands must be kept in front of oneself, which confirms the school of thought from the following century—hands on the table, arms crossed.

But most gestures still maintain a certain longevity, as is demonstrated by "The Behaviors of Paris," an eighteenth-century song that was accompanied by miming gestures:

> Ture, allure, allure,
> Flin, falan, faloan,
> Each has his own tone,
> And his own behavior.
>
> With this finger here (*the index*)
> A threat they will hear (*making a sign with the finger*).
> 'Tis like this we approve with respect (*nodding the head*),
> And like this that instead we reject (*furrowing the brow*),
> With this sign our favor we make plain (*holding out one's hand*),
> And like thus we display our disdain (*shrugging the shoulders*),
> A squeeze of the hand is the symbol of Friendship,
> With a kiss of the hand Eros flaunts his Courtship.
>
> Ture, allure, allure,
> Etc.
>
> When this gesture one presents
> An end is brought to events
> "*Ah, good sirs, a spot of quiet if you please.*"
> With this gesture here, peace you request (*crossing the hands*),
> And like thus, a secret is expressed (*a finger to the lips*).
> [...]
> To cry woe unto the skies
> One must only raise one's eyes.
> In praise of an item whose virtues we sing
> All five fingers to our lips we may bring
> "*How adorable!*"
> A gesture like this one shows our shame and disgrace (*joining the
>   hands together*)
> Whereas fear and concern have us double our pace,
> And Alas! we might say when it's pity we face,
> "*How I feel for you,*"
> Monotony, a stretch of the arms can erase.
> Ture, allure, allure,
> Etc.

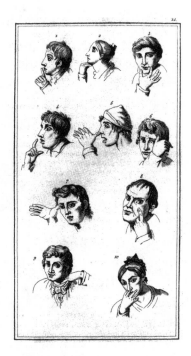

Andrea de Jorio, *La mimica degli antichi
investigata nel gestire napoletano*, Naples, 1832.

We would like to believe that these gestures and airs were at that
time those of the Parisians. In any case, they were unique enough
in the eyes of other Frenchmen that they warranted a song.

When he published *The Mime of the Ancients Investigated through
Neapolitan Gesture* in Naples in 1832, the Canon Andrea de Jorio
wanted to demonstrate that the gestures of the Neapolitans in use at
the time had ancient origins, which he had found on the amphorae
and paintings of antiquity. He proved to us, in any case, that the
gestures of the Neapolitans haven't changed over the past hundred
and seventy years.

But can gestures be classified? Alphabetical order must be
renounced (although certain gestures can already be found collected
in language dictionaries, such as the *bras d'honneur*, also known as
the "Italian salute"; the handshake; or "thumbing the nose"), and we

should instead successively address each part of the body, from top to bottom, from scalp to toe by way of the upper limbs.

Thus I have arranged into 37 sections nearly 850 descriptions of the gestures of the Western, Mediterranean, and Eastern worlds, accompanied by descriptive sketches, their meanings (which appear again in a general index), by any necessary verbal sign appended to them, and by literary citations. "Famous gestures" are illustrated by means of photographs or visual documents.

This *Dictionary of Gestures* has been subjected to the same restrictions as would any other dictionary of language in France, in that it is impossible to list exhaustively all technical and professional terminology, or terms from foreign languages, be they dead languages or living. As such, I have sought out neither the gestures used by sporting referees, nor those particular to the hard of hearing or the brokers of the stock exchange. This inventory would have surpassed the limits I had imposed upon myself, and would have in all certainty created confusion.

Owing to budgetary constraints, I also make no claims to an exhaustive inventory of international gestures, as I lacked the ability to pursue the travel that would have been necessary for such research. I have often had to content myself with the use of certain documentation, a list of which can be found in the bibliography.

Such as it is, this dictionary will be of as much interest to the semiotician as to the linguist. The inventory of this seventy-sixth French language should be seen as a supplement to those language dictionaries that, in an unassuming fashion, have attempted to reconcile word and gesture.

This demanding relationship has already been expressed by Henri Bergson. In *Laughter*, he wrote, "The perfect man, the style of whom would also be perfect, ought to have a different spontaneous gesture for each one of the expressions he employs."

Perhaps that is too much to ask. But it is true, seeing as with Bergson, it is a question of "style," that the gestures of communication are always voluntary—much as all literature is

voluntary—and we must leave the involuntary gestures, what the
Comte de Lautréamont referred to as the "tics, tics, and tics," to
the psychologists.

François Le Lionnais, the cofounder of the Oulipo with
Raymond Queneau, and to whom I had proposed some thirty years
ago that we combine our research, wrote to me on May 9, 1973:

> We will quite naturally need to make clear the role of "gestures" as far as
> the Third Sector is concerned.[1] Let us also not forget the duel that set Panurge
> against the Englishman and the manner in which he confounded him.

As you can see, this is a lovely example of the presence of gesture
in literature:

HOW PANURGE PUT TO A NONPLUS THE ENGLISHMAN THAT ARGUED BY SIGNS.
Everybody then taking heed, and hearkening with great silence, the Englishman
lift up on high into the air his two hands severally, clunching in all the tops of
his fingers together, after the manner which, a la Chinonnese, they call the hen's
arse, and struck the one hand on the other by the nails four several times. Then
he, opening them, struck the one with the flat of the other till it yielded a clashing
noise, and that only once. Again, in joining them as before, he struck twice, and
afterwards four times in opening them. Then did he lay them joined, and extended
the one towards the other, as if he had been devoutly to send up his prayers unto
God. Panurge suddenly lifted up in the air his right hand, and put the thumb
thereof into the nostril of the same side, holding his four fingers straight out,
and closed orderly in a parallel line to the point of his nose, shutting the left eye
wholly, and making the other wink with a profound depression of the eyebrows
and eyelids. Then lifted he up his left hand, with hard wringing and stretching
forth his four fingers and elevating his thumb, which he held in a line directly
correspondent to the situation of his right hand, with the distance of a cubit and
a half between them. This done, in the same form he abased towards the ground

---

1. François Le Lionnais's notion of the literary Third Sector expands on the
conceptualization of "paraliterature" as a Second Sector. Paraliterature classifies
written works such as genre fiction (detective fiction, science fiction, and fantasy,
westerns, etc.), comic books, romance novels, and the like, as being secondary
to primary sector literature. Accordingly, Third Sector literature expands on the
"socio-textual horizon," including general nonliterary works, advertising, jargons,
and technical writing, and particular to Le Lionnais's interests, "pharmaceutical
advertising, military punishment logs, and compendiums of tattoos and graffiti."
See Christophe Reig, *Mimer, miner, rimer: Le cycle romanesque de Jacques
Roubaud* (Amsterdam: Rodopi, 2006), chap. 3.—Trans.

about the one and the other hand. Lastly, he held them in the midst, as aiming right at the Englishman's nose. And if Mercury,—said the Englishman. There Panurge interrupted him, and said, You have spoken, Mask.

Then made the Englishman this sign. His left hand all open he lifted up into the air, then instantly shut into his fist the four fingers thereof, and his thumb extended at length he placed upon the gristle of his nose. Presently after, he lifted up his right hand all open, and all open abased and bent it downwards, putting the thumb thereof in the very place where the little finger of the left hand did close in the fist, and the four right-hand fingers he softly moved in the air. Then contrarily he did with the right hand what he had done with the left, and with the left what he had done with the right.

Panurge, being not a whit amazed at this, drew out into the air his trismegist codpiece with the left hand, and with his right drew forth a truncheon of a white ox-rib, and two pieces of wood of a like form, one of black ebony and the other of incarnation brasil, and put them betwixt the fingers of that hand in good symmetry; then, knocking them together, made such a noise as the lepers of Brittany use to do with their clappering clickets, yet better resounding and far

Illustration of Rabelais,
engraving by B. Picart, 1741.

more harmonious, and with his tongue contracted in his mouth did very merrily warble it, always looking fixedly upon the Englishman. The divines, physicians, and chirurgeons that were there thought that by this sign he would have inferred that the Englishman was a leper. The counsellors, lawyers, and decretalists conceived that by doing this he would have concluded some kind of mortal felicity to consist in leprosy, as the Lord maintained heretofore.

The Englishman for all this was nothing daunted, but holding up his two hands in the air, kept them in such form that he closed the three master-fingers in his fist, and passing his thumbs through his indical or foremost and middle fingers, his auriculary or little fingers remained extended and stretched out, and so presented he them to Panurge. Then joined he them so that the right thumb touched the left, and the left little finger touched the right. Hereat Panurge, without speaking one word, lift up his hands and made this sign.

He put the nail of the forefinger of his left hand to the nail of the thumb of the same, making in the middle of the distance as it were a buckle, and of his right hand shut up all the fingers into his fist, except the forefinger, which he often thrust in and out through the said two others of the left hand. Then stretched he out the forefinger and middle finger or medical of his right hand, holding them asunder as much as he could, and thrusting them towards Thaumast. Then did he put the thumb of his left hand upon the corner of his left eye, stretching out all his hand like the wing of a bird or the fin of a fish, and moving it very daintily this way and that way, he did as much with his right hand upon the corner of his right eye. Thaumast began then to wax somewhat pale, and to tremble, and made him this sign.

With the middle finger of his right hand he struck against the muscle of the palm or pulp which is under the thumb. Then put he the forefinger of the right hand in the like buckle of the left, but he put it under, and not over, as Panurge did. Then Panurge knocked one hand against another, and blowed in his palm, and put again the forefinger of his right hand into the overture or mouth of the left, pulling it often in and out. Then held he out his chin, most intentively looking upon Thaumast. The people there, which understood nothing in the other signs, knew very well that therein he demanded, without speaking a word to Thaumast, What do you mean by that? In effect, Thaumast then began to sweat great drops, and seemed to all the spectators a man strangely ravished in high contemplation. Then he bethought himself, and put all the nails of his left hand against those of his right, opening his fingers as if they had been semicircles, and with this sign lift up his hands as high as he could. Whereupon Panurge presently put the thumb of his right hand under his jaws, and the little finger thereof in the mouth of the left hand, and in this posture made his teeth to sound very melodiously, the upper against the lower. With this Thaumast, with great toil and vexation of spirit, rose up, but in rising let a great baker's fart, for the bran came after, and pissing withal very strong vinegar, stunk like all the devils in hell. The company began to stop their noses; for he had conskited himself with mere anguish and perplexity. Then lifted he up his right hand, clunching it in such sort that he brought the ends of all his fingers to meet together, and his left hand he laid flat upon his breast. Whereat Panurge drew out his long codpiece with his tuff, and stretched it forth a cubit and a half, holding it in the air with his right hand, and with his left took out his orange, and, casting it up into the air seven times, at the eighth he hid it in the fist of his right hand, holding it steadily up on high, and then began to shake his fair codpiece, showing it to Thaumast.

After that, Thaumast began to puff up his two cheeks like a player on a bagpipe, and blew as if he had been to puff up a pig's bladder. Whereupon Panurge put one finger of his left hand in his nockandrow, by some called St. Patrick's hole, and with his mouth sucked in the air, in such a manner as when one eats oysters in the shell, or when we sup up our broth. This done, he opened his mouth somewhat, and struck his right hand flat upon it, making therewith a great and a deep sound, as if it came from the superficies of the midriff through the trachiartery or pipe of the lungs, and this he did for sixteen times; but Thaumast did always keep blowing like a goose. Then Panurge put the forefinger of his right hand into his mouth, pressing it very hard to the muscles thereof; then he drew it out, and withal made a great noise, as when little boys shoot pellets out of the pot-cannons made of the hollow sticks of the branch of an alder-tree, and he did it nine times.

Then Thaumast cried out, Ha, my masters, a great secret! With this he put in his hand up to the elbow, then drew out a dagger that he had, holding it by the point downwards. Whereat Panurge took his long codpiece, and shook it as hard as he could against his thighs; then put his two hands entwined in manner of a comb upon his head, laying out his tongue as far as he was able, and turning his eyes in his head like a goat that is ready to die. Ha, I understand, said Thaumast, but what? making such a sign that he put the haft of his dagger against his breast, and upon the point thereof the flat of his hand, turning in a little the ends of his fingers. Whereat Panurge held down his head on the left side, and put his middle finger into his right ear, holding up his thumb bolt upright. Then he crossed his two arms upon his breast and coughed five times, and at the fifth time he struck his right foot against the ground. Then he lift up his left arm, and closing all his fingers into his fist, held his thumb against his forehead, striking with his right hand six times against his breast. But Thaumast, as not content therewith, put the thumb of his left hand upon the top of his nose, shutting the rest of his said hand, whereupon Panurge set his two master-fingers upon each side of his mouth, drawing it as much as he was able, and widening it so that he showed all his teeth, and with his two thumbs plucked down his two eyelids very low, making therewith a very ill-favoured countenance, as it seemed to the company.

François Rabelais, *The Works of Rabelais*, Book II, trans. Thomas Urquhart, 1653

This lengthy dialogue in gestures by François Rabelais is unique in French literature; but writers have always enjoyed the description of gestures. Here is how Kafka recounted the tale of an accident as mimed by one of his protagonists:

It is first a question of explaining how the accident happened. The motor-car owner with raised palms simulates the approaching motor-car; he sees the tricycle cutting across his path, detaches his right hand, and gesticulates back and forth in warning to it, a worried expression on his face—what motor-car could apply its brakes in time in so short a distance? Will the tricycle understand this and give the motor-car the right of way? No, it is too late; his left hand ceases its warning motions, both hands join together for the collision, his knees bend to watch the last moments. It has happened, and the bent, motionless tricycle standing there can now assist in the description.

Franz Kafka, *The Diaries: 1910–1923*, trans. Joseph Kresh, 1948

Other writers have preferred to suggest gestures without
describing them:

The King, weary from having created one librarian for every book in the entire
expanse of his kingdom, began to grow tired of all the cosmopolitan verbiage of
which he never understood a thing. He bid them to explain themselves with clarity
and to find him, as rapidly as possible, the means of acquiring the beauty he so
desired, or failing that. ... I dare not say by which terrible gesture the king's words
were accompanied, but the poor learned men all trembled with a noise like that of
shaken old medallions, and finding once again, with a burst of great emotion, the
use of their mother tongue, they promised it would be so, beset as they were by the
greatest of anxieties.

Henry Somm, "A Tale to Drive Young Children Mad," *Le Chat Noir*,
January 20, 1883

Or, even more succinctly:

"The Saint-Chapelle (silence) (gesture) that gem of Gothic art (gesture) (silence)."

Raymond Queneau, *Zazie in the Metro*, trans. Barbara Wright, 1960

Raymond Queneau does not describe the gestures. The noneffusive
Normand only points out their existence in the dialogue of his
novel's characters, but nothing more: for him, the words are what is
important; the gesture is nothing but punctuation.

These literary gestures allow us to ask ourselves if they perhaps
possess a grammar and a syntax of their own, in the same way that
written words do. Without going too far into it, we can already
remark that the gesture has a grammatical tense, which is the
present of the indicative: one makes a gesture, even if the use of
the imperative (a request for someone to get lost, for example)
foresees a future. In this case, the gesture is simply the invitation;
it is not the act.

During the course of my research, each time I asked someone
to name for me the people who gesticulate the most, I was first
told the Italians ... followed by the Native Americans. Similarly, it
was remarked that French gestures are less emphatic than, say,
the gestures of the Neapolitans. It is known that Mediterraneans
"speak with their hands" and that the English are instead
"phlegmatic"—both of which opinions are relative to the gestures

of Parisians. Just as a language has a lexical stress pattern, gestures have one as well, which can lead to difficulties of comprehension between peoples.

He spoke with his entire mouth like the French, with many gestures like the English, with his shoulders like an Italian, and all of this put together in a German.
   Georg Lichtenberg, *The Mirror of the Soul*

From there, we are tempted to seek out the origins, for lack of a possible etymology, because of the extent to which certain gestures make it seem that there must be a cultural core that most of the time eludes us. I prudently made note of few interpretations that, if they are in no way certain, at least present some originality.

   We must nevertheless recognize that certain gestures are disappearing or no longer appear save under the guise of graphic fossils—such as the kiss of the hand, which I preserved out of consideration for President Jacques Chirac, who made regular use of it. The gestures of cooling oneself with a fan or of carrying a parasol in the summer have become uncommon, as have

La voilette, illustrated supplement of *Le Journal*.

the objects themselves—or at least they have in France, where furthermore we have lost the gesture of raising the veil, which women no longer wear, a gesture to be compared culturally to that of veiled women in the Muslim world.

French President Jacques Chirac greets
US Secretary of State Condoleezza Rice, Paris, France,
January 25, 2007. US Department of State photo.

We might also remark that aggressive gestures have a tendency to follow the same progression as verbal violence. Obscene gestures, which were used with restraint until fairly recently, have become commonplace in the schoolyard, and so prevalent that women now use them as much as men.

PUBLIC GESTURES

Much as there are different levels of language, there are different levels of gestural expression. The people this affects most, given that eloquence tends to disappear in favor of a rhetoric of televisual communication, are actors. Whichever stage they perform on—mimes, Italian-style theater, street performance, movies, television—they each have their own gestures.

Although the following is a departure from the limited gestural domain of our inventory, it is interesting to consider the reflections of Georges Polti in regard to the notation of gestures he had undertaken. Here, we will see that a taste for precision can go quite far:

If we are to consider the human forms before us as they move—a spectacle that quickly becomes delightful—we perceive, in the *head*, the *body*, and the *limbs*, the three principal groups of the orchestra of movements. Each of the four limbs can be divided in turn into three parts (arm, forearm, and hand; thigh, leg, and foot). And finally the extremity, be it leg or foot, of a limb, reproduces this triple division in the phalanges of each of its five fingers or toes.

And the subdivision into mobile parts stops definitively at that third degree. For one of these fractions we have already indicated (be it a forearm, or a thigh, or a phalanx, etc.) cannot be divided into others susceptible to being bent one against the other, in the way the forearm folds back against the arm, the thigh against the body, the nail-bearing phalanx against the medial phalanx, etc. This phalanx, this thigh, this forearm, etc., taken separately, forms in this way an inflexible element: it can do no more than move around its point of attachment (incidentally carrying with it in its movements the object or other element that can be found fixed to its free extremity); all in all it is a sort of radius, variable in exterior form, but still, a rigid radius that moves around a point of attachment.

At the outset (that's to say, in the instant immediately preceding the one when we begin to take note of the gestures of our actor), we must suppose that it is in a state of rigid comportment like that of an Egyptian mummy, the head straight, eyes and lips closed, arms along the body with the palms of the hands glued to the sides of the thighs, and the two feet together from heel to toe.

Each of the spheres where the movement of each of the mobile elements of this whole is to take place, we first divide it into *latitudes*; these latitudes are the degrees to which the vertical movements must elevate and lower themselves; they will be indicated by the ordinary lowercase letters. These indications begin at the initial point and increase in front of the individual and then redescend, at the back, finally rejoining the starting point; there are in all twelve degrees. Similarly, twelve *longitudes* are the degrees through which the horizontal movements pass; these, upon leaving their initial point, spread apart in front and toward the outside in order to return, from the rear and toward the inside, to their starting point. The longitudes will be indicated by *italicized* lowercase letters. Twelve analogous letters taken from the Greek alphabet will similarly serve for the degrees of the sphere delineated by the members turning on their own axes.

By combining for each mobile part the diverse types of movements to which they are susceptible, we obtain very large numbers: 441 for the head, for example; but in reality there are only roughly 200 possible positions for the head (without mentioning, of course, the innumerable nuances obtained by means of the many subdivisions that we can mark, as we have said, by adding Arabic numbers to the letters). Of the 930 combinations imaginable for the shoulders (considering them both at once and each in their own positions), there are really only 400 or 500 which are feasible. Of the 125 postures of the body, we would hardly be able to count as far as 100.

Of the 178 of the arm, there are only 130 that are possible; but, combined in all sorts of ways with the 18 of the forearm and the 64 possible to the fist (of 75), that would allow more than 160,000 gestures for the arm as a whole. However, as each of those three controls in some way the other two and restrains their play, not even a tenth of those gestures of the whole are feasible; which still allows for quite an impressive number.

We can count nearly 200 varied comportments for the Thigh, of the roughly 300 we are able to imagine based on the preceding givens; 18 for the leg itself, and 58 (of 72) for the foot. It is thus again in the tens of thousands that we could count for the movements of the lower limbs. [...]

Considering nothing but the hand, if we were to take the 240 principal configurations of the thumb (alongside which there are another 60 which are unachievable), the 61 of the other base phalanges, the 20 of the medial phalanges, and the 20 of the nail-bearing phalanges, and multiply all of them together, we would arrive at over *8 million* of these positions of the hand that so pleased Watteau, and of which at least 5 million are at once easy to achieve and very distinct in style.

And it is by the tens of thousands once again that we could enumerate the forms presented by the foot in movement. Who would believe it, to see depicted, unconscious and unmoved upon the great works of our statuary, this marvelous member, who alone tells the trace of the passing of a race upon the Earth, and of whom Greek physiognomy had made one of the most important seats of its remarks!

Georges Polti, *Notation des gestes* (The notation of gestures), 1893

Not unlike actors, singers on stage for the most part present "false" gestures. Without even considering the difficulty lyrical singers demonstrate in bringing together the bel canto and expressive gestures, we can see that certain popular singers, and not the least of them, make no gestures whatsoever on stage other than strumming a guitar, and remain "wooden," whereas the cabaret singers from a hundred years ago made an effort to adopt the characteristic gestures of their trade, and dancing girls who made use of the whole stage were not uncommon. Perhaps gestures are generally more useful in close communication, and from afar, from the stage, it is necessary to "throw" them so that they reach the public.

The choreographic arts are an art of the gesture par excellence, and it would be useful for us to inventory the oriental dances that made such an impact on enthusiasts and dancers alike during the Universal Expositions of 1889 and 1900, and during the Colonial Exposition of 1931, before closer connections between nations were later established.

The eloquence of preachers, lawyers, and politicians has, from time immemorial, made as much use of gestures as it has of speech. Demosthenes stated that each of them had the same importance. As for some of the judges at the Areopagus, they were

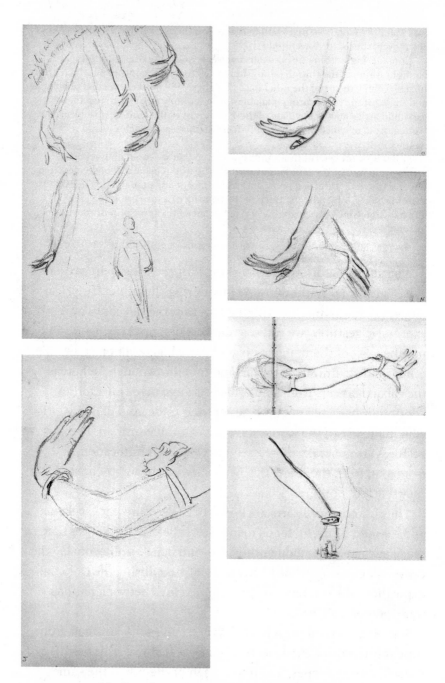

John Singer Sargent, *Javanese Dancer, Hand and Arm Positions*
(from *Sketchbook of Javanese Dancers*, 1889). The Metropolitan Museum of Art.

Four women dancers in Javanese Village, full-length portrait, standing, in costume, Paris Exposition, 1889. Image from Library of Congress, Prints and Photographs Division, LOT 6634, no. 287.

so wary of the orators' gestures, or so it is said, that they preferred to listen to them in the dark so as not to be influenced by them.

The French illustrator Christophe (Marie Louise Georges Colomb, 1856–1945) successfully grasped the gestures of Master Bafouillet, the defense for *Camember the Sapper* (in 1893), whereas Steinlein, at roughly the same time, recaps in *Le Chat Noir* the gestures made by Rudolphe Salis as he commented on *L'Épopéé*, Caran d'Ache's projection onto the screen of the shadow theater brought to life by Henri Rivière.

In the seventeenth century, the Reverend Father Sanlec (whose verse was collected in 1693 by the Reverend Father Bouhours) penned a long rhyming tirade published under the title *The Art of Preaching, or On Gesture*, from which I have pulled two excerpts, from the beginning and the end:

Comments by Rodolphe Salis.
Illustration by C. Léandre.

'Tis in vain for a priest when he preaches the Good Book
To blend pleasant and useful with his most Christian hook:
If he adds no fine gesture to his art of oration,
If in all his appearance there is no filiation,
His voice will charm no longer, his phrase convey no story;
From the outset do I toil toward eternal glory;
Should I sometimes grow weary, in my speech lack conviction,
I will awake with a start when is reached benediction.
So you whom to preach travels the wide Earth to determine
How best to gather a crowd to encircle your sermon;
Would you create a demand for all your benches and pews,
And for the heavenly gates have your flock so enthuse?
[...]
I know in our parishes immodest fools whose worst crimes
Lie in replacing one word by gesturing ninety times;
I have heard others as well whom I must also bemoan,
Who choose one hundred wrong words over one gesture alone:
But for gesture and meaning, parallel measure must grant
That one's eye they enrapture just as one's ear they enchant.
And if gesture and meaning they must as partners conspire,
The sense of one right word a gesture will never acquire.
Above all do not act like those men denuded of charms
Who mimic the pendulum carelessly dangling their arms
Do not force them to see you through your hands in their flailing;

And never speak like you'd share in the parlor your railing.
With the new kind of Actors it has become quite the craze
For them to swim all about each time they've ended a phrase.
Among those who're just learning it may seem entertaining
For them to write in the air, and in speech to be painting.
The former with just one hand seems to incense the faithful,
The latter, his hooked fingers appear frozen and painful.
This one here likes exposing bare arms for all to behold,
That one there's pantomiming, counting his silver and gold.
And this clumsy speaker's arm, he'll never put it to use,
And that one's widespread fingers like the webbed feet of a goose.
Often charmed by the meaning of what I say to the crowd
I even applaud myself, clapping my hands hard and loud.
Sometimes I hope that never shall my sentences run dry,
I will tell them I am done, bring my hand down on my thigh.
There are times when my spirit can reckon nothing brighter,
And although it's well in place, I straighten up my miter.
On occasion I let loose a very thunderous voice
As I play the timpanist on my pulpit and rejoice.

On the 22 Haha of 78 E.P., the *Cahiers of the Collège de Pataphysique* published the following in their nos. 3–4, *The 31 Positions of R. F. Ravignan*, presented by Abbot A. Girard, the vicar of Notre-Dame de la Croix de Ménilmontant:

The reading of this text must be scrupulously accompanied by the gestures described.

1. EXPOSITION—Right arm front, half circle. It is suitable to begin thus the first words of the exordium.
2. ENUMERATION OF OPPOSITIONS (HERE, THERE, TO ONE SIDE, TO THE OTHER)—Arm straight to the left, then to the right.
3. EXCLAMATION—Eyes and arms raised skyward.
4. COMPASSION—Hands joined together on the left, or fully splayed but held somewhat lower. Head leaned to the left.
5. ?
6. HORROR—Right arm in front and to the right, head turned to the left, sometimes only the left hand or else both arms turned to the right.
7. AFFIRMATION—Right arm forward, the hand in a horizontal position, palm turned toward the audience.
8. INTERDICTION, COMMANDMENT—Right arm outstretched, fingers closed except for the index, hand tilted.
9. FOR EMPHASIS—Right arm curved, fingers closed, index at top.
10. CONTEMPT—Right arm abruptly to the left, or only the left hand.
11. ADMIRATION—Arms slightly raised, the eyes as well, gaze fixed.
12. QUESTIONING—Right arm forward, sometimes with a slight wavering to the hand.

13. FEAR, DREAD—Body leaned slightly back, arms making a sort of cross, palms of the hands toward the audience.

14. INDICATION (OBSERVE, GENTLEMEN)—Right arm forward if it is positive, to the left if it is negative, and if so, the head leaning slightly to the right. When it is a question of something sad, pitiful, the two arms are either to the left or in front, but lowered.

15. ADJURATION (I BEG OF YOU)—Arms forward, head leaning slightly to the right.

16. OPPOSITION—Right arm held forward, hand in a vertical position.

17. ACT OF REVERSAL—Sudden movement of the arm, from right to left.

18. ACT OF BREAKING, OF DESTROYING—The arms in the same direction.

19. GREATNESS—Arms up in a slight circle.

20. AUGMENTATION—Arms gradually loosened away from the body and hands making light undulations.

21. ACT OF LAGGING BEHIND—Right arm moving slowly from left to right.

22. IRONY—Right arm slightly forward, slight movement of the right hand and the head, sometimes turned in the opposite direction, or, the hand gesture (19) with an ironic tone and smile.

23. TIME PASSED—Right arm to the left; present, right arm in front of oneself, slightly to the right; to come, right arm slightly behind the right shoulder.

24. DISTANCE—Right arm stretched out, finger pointing.

25. TRIUMPH, VICTORY, JOY—Right arm quickly drawing a sort of parabola, starting at the middle of the chest and moving upwards, sometimes both arms at once.

26. ACT OF DEPICTING, RECOUNTING—Right arm, fingers splayed.

27. WISHES, PLAINTIVENESS—Hands crossed over the chest, or arms spread wide.

28. TO DESIGNATE THE HEART—Hand reached over the left side of the chest, fingers turned under at a right angle to the belt.

29. DESPONDENCY, SADNESS—Head leaning, arms as if overcome, right hand carelessly pressed against the left.

30. CONCERN, ACTION OF DESERVING—The arm deployed from the heart forward.

31. BUT, HOWEVER—The index alone hooked, or the arm, but up.

The manner in which an orator of antiquity enumerated successive arguments offers us a transition: the orator deploys the five fingers of his hand, then successively closes one, two, three, four fingers over the palm and finishes with a closed fist; he then opens it by successively raising one, two, three, four, and finally all five fingers of the hand.

Before we launch into the art of counting with the fingers, let us first begin with a clownish entry. The white clown is addressing the auguste:

Eloquence of the robe.
(*Camember the Sapper.*)

You want to make a bet? I bet that you have eleven fingers! Hold your hands up, I will prove to you that you have eleven. (*He first counts the fingers of the left hand, then those of the right hand.*) Ten ... Nine ... Eight ... Seven ... Six ... One ... Two ... Three ... Four ... Five ... Six and five make eleven. I win!

Not everyone counts on their fingers the same way. Europeans start counting with the thumb (one), Americans with the index (one). For the Japanese, the thumb is 5. (More details can be found in section 22, which is devoted to the hand.) In Europe, 1 (the thumb), 2 (thumb + index), 3 (thumb + index + middle), 4 (thumb + index + middle + ring finger), 5 (all five fingers). In the United States, 1 (index), 2 (index + middle), 3 (index + middle + ring), 4 (index + middle + ring + little finger), 5 (all five fingers).

Counting with the fingers can sometimes lead to surprises, like the three fingers a referee placed inadvertently on his thigh during

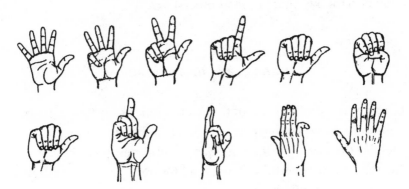

Counting in sign language, classical antiquity.

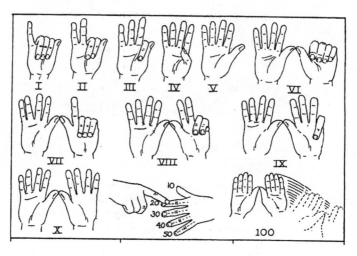

Counting in sign language, India.

a televised soccer match in 1997, which elicited from the player a response that was appropriate to the situation ...

As early as the seventh century, we made use of the computus of Ruban Maur (or the pseudo-Isidore of Seville), for which we use the phalanges of both hands (thus twenty-eight) to form the numbers. Today, more frequently we settle for using the fist to help memorize the days of the months of the year (see further on, description 22.111).

The symbolism of numbers can be closely related to gestures. Thus the drawing of the Cross (forehead, chest, left shoulder, right shoulder) follows that of the number 4.

THE SECRET OF GESTURES

To recent recruit Pitanchu of the second unit of the first regiment, wanting as he was to have free entrance to the theater where "the play they were performing was a brand-new piece which Freemasons were permitted to attend for free," Camember the Sapper said the following:

All you have to do is present yourself to the people who are behind a sort of counter, and you sign in with them using the gesture I am currently demonstrating to you. It's the gesture the Freemasons use when they want to go see the Tour de Nesle ... and they will let you straight in.

And the Sapper teaches the recruit to hit himself on the back of his neck with his left hand, his right hand dangling under the nose of his interlocutor, his tongue stuck out to him. Alas, the gesture must have been misunderstood, because the recruit neglected to wear gloves, and when that happens, the gesture, at the drop of a hat, means: "You, sir, are a dingbat!"

So often coded gestures risk being misinterpreted by the uninitiated ... Even before Christophe, Edgar Allan Poe shows his astonishment at a gesture, which he describes in *The Cask of Amontillado*:

I broke and reached him a flagon of De Grave. He emptied it in a breath. His eyes flashed with a fierce light. He laughed and threw the bottle upwards with a gesticulation I did not understand.

I looked at him in surprise. He repeated the movement—a grotesque one.

"You do not comprehend?" he said.

"Not I," I replied.

"Then you are not of the brotherhood."

"How?"

"You are not of the masons."

Christophe,
Camember the Sapper.

The same astonishment can be found in *The Words* by
Jean-Paul Sartre:

> He resembled Vincent Auriol, and my grandfather maintained that he was a
> third-degree mason. "When I say hello to him," he told us, with the frightened
> repulsion of a good citizen to whom a homosexual is making advances,
> "he makes the masonic triangle with his thumb on the palm of my hand."
>
> Jean-Paul Sartre, *The Words*, trans. Bernard Frechtman, 1964

As long as the French "Compagnons" guilds and the Masons
have existed, the illustrated weeklies—the direction and editorial
boards of which are not without representatives of Freemasonry—
have taken joy in revealing, at least once a year, the Masons'
signs of greeting. Here are a few of them, pulled from various
recent weeklies:

To signify that he would prefer death to the revelation of secrets,
the apprentice places his right hand under his throat, the four
fingers clutched together, the thumb out at a right angle, and
feigns to slit his own throat before letting his hand fall.

The Compagnon performs the same gesture, but level with the
heart. The master makes the same gesture, but with the hand
placed on the left side of the stomach.

The sign of horror at the thought of the death of Hiram has
been borrowed from the orators of antiquity: it's the recoil of the
head and shoulders.

And finally, the sign of Masonic distress, which is the same as
that of the Legionnaires, accompanied by a cry of "O Lord, is there
no help for the Widow's son?" or "To me, Legion!": hands joined
together, fingers interlaced, palms turned upward. This symbol
often appears in the traditional novel, to which it adds a little spice.

The exchange of secrets takes place face to face, heads leaning
toward each other, the right hand placed on the left shoulder of the
interlocutor, who does the same, while the two initiates whisper
the password after having kissed each other's cheeks three times.

The touching of the hands, which often make noninitiates
shudder: the apprentice presses on the index finger of his
interlocutor three times; to these three squeezes, the Compagnon

adds two more on the middle finger; with the masters, the hands are interlaced, the index and the middle finger pressing on the fist of the brother.

These revelations have never really seemed to bother the Freemasons ...

Also well known, thanks to popular engravings, are what the Compagnons of the Tour de France refer to as *guilebrettes*, who demonstrate their fraternity as they drink by crossing their arms with those of another Compagnon.

The "chains" of union and brotherhood have spread widely outside of the lodges and make up a type of diplomatic game during the meetings of heads of state, especially when it comes time for the family photograph.

In the early 1960s, André Martel, French writer and Regent of the Collège de Pataphysique, also known as the "Papapafol of the

Guilebrettes.

Paralloïdre," created an "occult salutation" for the *Parapotes* (or Parapals) in nine stages, with the same number of finger positions being performed with the hands. Parapals being quite rare, their secret has not spread far.

All secret societies have their own rituals, their symbols and their signs of recognition, as Georges Perec described in *53 Days*:

> The structures and methods of the BH [Black Hand] are borrowed from various secret societies—the Sicilian mafia, the Camorra in Naples, the Doriani of Bari, the Fiscalrassi of Montenegro. Its members are called *mortaretti*—an Italian word (there have always been significant Italian and Maltese minorities in Grianta) originally meaning "a small mortar," but which actually refers to the sawn-off shot-guns which most BH members use. They generally act in groups of five, called a "hand": four "fingers" and a leader, the "thumb," four "thumbs" are led by a "number one thumb," four "number one thumbs" are under a "big thumb." Above big thumb level, the organisation awards sonorous titles to those who are near to the apex of the pyramid—"knight," "commander," "first master," "master," "grandmaster."
>
> Georges Perec, *53 Days*, trans. David Bellos, 1992

Also, periodically but less consistently than when it comes to Freemasonry, young black Americans have been discussed in the French press, which, for the most part, has only been reprinting translated articles that first appeared in the United States. Thus, in 1995, the war and subsequent peace between the Crips and the Bloods in Los Angeles was an opportunity to describe their hand signs of solidarity to the world.

Perfectly honorable professions, discreet perhaps, but never secret, also have their own particular codes: the stock exchange, the bustle of which is always entertaining to see; the fish-hawkers in the fishing ports (whose winks have begun to disappear since electronic bidding has become more and more widespread); auction houses also have their own codes, which are good to know before one begins to bid.

All of these professions—and the English bookmakers of the racetrack—use gestures in the same way that Chappe's tachygraph did, which transmitted information by the waving of arms.

Of course, we cannot forget the gestures of sports referees, which differ from sport to sport, the gestures of marine navigation and diving, of transportation and public works, of firemen, parachutists, landing procedures at airports, and so on.

The last secret gestures we might point out are those of thieves and gamblers, which we more pleasantly refer to as collusion signaling.

[In 1928,] in the shop run by Laperche, a new goods seller in Rue Saint-Denis, three shawl scarves were stolen. The two women were spotted sharing complicit signals.

Y. Lemoine, *Crimes of Paris*

It is among these, pulled from real life, that we find traces of the signals referred to in French argot as the *serre* or the *serbillon*, which slang dictionaries attest back as far as 1835. The etymology of this gesture's name is obscure and fanciful. The most likely option is the verb *serrer* in the jargon of the gambler: *serrer son jeu* is to conceal one's cards, to not let them be seen; so *jouer serré* is to act with prudence. *Serre*, then, is a noun derived from an imperative verb, much like "cover" or "pocket." In any case, this is a "covert" gesture (*covert* in turn being derived from the past participle of the Old French verb *covrir* ["to cover"]), similar in meaning to the English expression "to hold one's cards close to one's chest."

SILENT GESTURES

French sign language (LSF) has nothing in common with the gestures of those without hearing difficulties: it is a language in and of itself that makes use of one or both hands, with their movements taking place in three dimensions. It is capable of expressing both concrete images and the subtleties of abstraction.

Dactylology can more plainly be described as a visualization code for the letters of the alphabet, as invented by a Spaniard,

Juan Pablo Bonet, in 1620, which was followed in the nineteenth century by the alphabet devised by French Abbot Charles-Michel de l'Épée; this alphabet is complementary to the LSF, and is used in the expression of proper names and their spelling. But it can also be used by jokers:

A MIMED ARTICLES

Monsieur Henri Rochefort, wanting to symbolize the freedom which, according to him, the new laws permitted, resorted to the following process. He paid for a page to be published in the *Intransigeant*, which, as a feature article, included a column filled with small line drawings representing hands making the gestures used in the language of deaf-mutes. Below, the signature "Henri Rochefort." Ingenious newsmen, as they hawked the *Intransigeant*, sold at the same time to its readers the deaf-mute alphabet, through which the readers could decode the rebus. The fun was over with quickly, and the readers were left very disappointed; underneath Monsieur Rochefort's inventive writing, they found nothing more than these two average lines of verse:

> Republicans, here is the guillotine;
> Tonight at the Élysée there will be dancing,

from which it is difficult to grasp the allusion to the then-current circumstances. In any case, his project was sufficient to "annoy" the administration for several hours; this was, most likely, the only thing Monsieur Rochefort set out to do.

Revue Encyclopédique, Larousse, 1894, "Revue" section, 267

Muteness is not always involuntary. Men who have withdrawn into monasteries and taken a vow of silence have substituted for their speech a somewhat rudimentary system of sign language. "From the medieval era, we still know of the shorter nomenclature of Ulrich, introduced in 1083, which involves only 52 signs, and the longer one, that of William of Hirsau, from the end of the eleventh century, which comprises 365 signs."[2] This relative poverty of language is intentional, as in strict observation of the rules of Saint Benedict, it was inappropriate for the monks to break their vow of silence by a "chattering" of signs. In the same spirit, these monastic signs are as limited as possible to a single hand; when a lone finger is enough to convey the meaning, the index finger is always used.

2. Aude de Saint-Loup, Yves Delaporte, and Marc Renard, *Gestes des moines, regards des sourds* (Siloë, 1997).

From John Bulwer,
Chirologia, or the Natural Language of the Hand
(London, 1644).

Another language we are familiar with is that of the Native Americans. These signs have long been studied by the Americans themselves, and there is no shortage of books on the subject.

Beautiful organ music. The gestures of the preacher. Dance and ritual. Gesture—(a phrase from Guénon that had greatly confounded me: and that I'm still not certain I understand). A certain fervor. Elation, even.

Raymond Queneau, *Journal*, July 22, 1940

It was not possible for me to undertake an exhaustive inventory of religious gestures, the gestures of both the priests and the

Examples of *mudras* or ritual gestures in Buddhism.

faithful from the various known rituals. Still, further on you will nonetheless find the most common ones, from the sign of the Cross to prostration on one's stomach upon the ground.

HAND GAMES

The gestures of the hand appear in numerous games. The best known is *morra*, known in France as *le jeu de la mourre*, which was already being played in Ancient Egypt. The two players raise their fist and bring it down, opening at the same time a certain number of fingers and shouting out the number of their bet as to how much the sum of the two fists will be. It is only in appearance a game of chance, because cheating is frequent and the game often degenerates into altercations. To such a point that the Romans extolled the integrity of a man by saying, "He is so honest that you could play morra with him in the dark."

Georges Soulié de Morant recounts in his *Bijou de Ceinture* that, before the Revolution of 1911, in Peking,

A game of *morra*.

The rich merchants of this opulent city, at the end of their day of labor, only rarely went to see a show. Instead, they preferred to gather in restaurants with glaring lights, and lingered, playing at "guessing the fists," *tchaé tiuann*, a kind of *morra* where you try to predict the total number of fingers splayed out or closed on the right hand, which the two players would throw at the same time, each of them crying out what he thought would be the number formed by his folded-back fingers and those of his antagonist.

A similar game is the one played in the schoolyards of France. The players throw out their hands at the same time, using the following gestures:

PAPER: the hand stretched out, the palm turned toward the ground.
SCISSORS: the index and middle fingers stretched out and apart from each other, the others adjoining the palm.
ROCK: the fist closed.
WELL: the thumb and the index finger form a ring, which the other fingers extend into a cylinder.

The rules of the game are as follows. A player earns a point when he has formed an object that is "stronger" than the one formed by his adversary. If two same objects are formed simultaneously, the turn is a tie. The hierarchy of objects is determined by the following relations:

PAPER is cut by scissors, plugs the well, and covers rock.
SCISSORS cut the paper, are broken by the rock, and fall into the well.
ROCK breaks the scissors, falls into the well, and is covered by paper.
THE WELL swallows paper and scissors, and is plugged up by the paper.

The game of *hot hands* is another well-known game. A player, blindfolded, kneeling down with his hands open behind his back, palms up, must guess who has given him a slap on the hand.

In the *wet finger* game, a child, after having moistened one of his fingers, presents them to his friend for him to choose one; the one to choose the wet finger is the winner—or loser, according to the rules agreed on beforehand.

Of course, the toy aisle has many childish games involving the fingers: *marionettes*, about which a French song has been shown to go back as far as the fifteenth century; a French tickling game for children called *The Little Bug That Climbs*, another called *Je te tiens par la barbichette*, the song that translates as "I've got you by your little goatee," and plenty of others learned in daycare and kindergarten.

In the schoolyard, hand games can also sometimes be naughty games, such as these two noted by Claude Gaignebet, in his *The Obscene Folklore of Children*.

STORY NO. 1
"If she hadn't done this"
(*spread apart the middle and index fingers and keep the others tight to the palm of the hand*)
"when she saw this"
(*the fist closed tight, push the tip of the thumb out from between the two first phalanges of the index and ring fingers*"
"she wouldn't have got this"
(*open the hand*)
Translation: If she hadn't spread her legs, when she saw an erect member, she wouldn't have had five children.

STORY NO. 2
"Jeannette heads into the woods"
(*the middle and index fingers move on a plane, imitating walking legs, the other fingers are closed in a fist*)
"she runs into (boy's name)"
(*the palm of the hand turned upward, the fingers closed with the exception of the middle finger, which is perpendicular to the plane of the palm*)
"she comes out like this"
(*same gesture as the first, only the "legs" must appear to be farther apart.*)
Translation: Jeannette goes into the woods a virgin; there she meets X with an erection; she leaves having been deflowered.

Among adults, "humorous stories" involving gestures are not very common. Here is one:

"Would you like a glass of port, Ma'am?
"Just a finger."
"Yes, but first, wouldn't you like a glass of port?"

The humorist and singer François Chevais would perform, in the cabarets of the 1950s and 1960s, what he referred to as a *chanson de geste*, or "gesture song." He would sing "La Mer" (The sea) by Charles Trenet, miming along with it in gestural plays-on-words:

La mer (the sea): he would make as if to rock a baby to sleep—from *la mère* (the mother)

qu'on voit (that we see): gesture of two fists forming a pair of binoculars in front of the eyes

danser (dancing): undulating gesture with the hand

le long des golfes clairs (all along the well-lit gulfs): he would simulate swinging a golf club—from the verb *golfer* (to golf)

a des reflets d'argent (has glints of silver): he would rub the thumb against the index finger—from *argent* (money), etc.

In the cabarets and music halls, we also shouldn't forget the other "player of hands," the illusionist, whose gestures relate more to dexterity than they do to communication.

Let us finish this overview with *ombromanie*, otherwise known as *shadowgraphy*:

In a column entitled "Things to Do on Rainy Thursdays," our children's magazines were always giving illustrated explanations of the way to go about it. But however hard we tried, no matter how we twisted our fingers, we never observed any progress from one time to the next. The duck looked just like the dog, the donkey like the rabbit, the elephant had to make do with a dangling forefinger for a trunk, and the camel lost count of its humps. As for the Indian chief, the only human being in our fabulous menagerie, his feathered headdress composed of five outstretched fingers made him look like a pincushion. In the end, we fell back on what we did best: the bird, which simply consisted of crossing your thumbs and clapping your hands to make slowly flapping wings. An indefinable bird, but at least it had the merit of taking flight when we stretched out our arms, like a dove that has just appeared out of a sleeve.

Jean Rouaud, *Of Illustrious Men*, trans. Barbara Wright, 1994

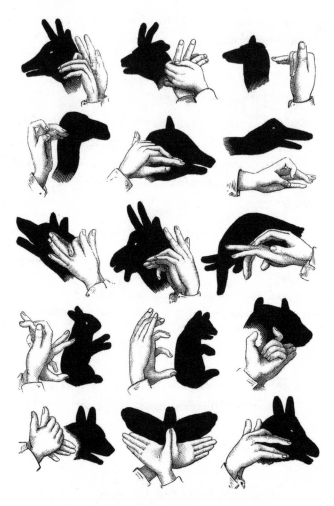

From *Cassell's Complete Book of Sports and Pastimes:
Being a Compendium of Out-door and In-door Amusements*
(London: Cassell, 1896).

Tom Tit, the author of *La Science amusante* (Amusing science),
three volumes bound in red and gold published by Larousse in 1890,
shows some other examples. A more recent book by Hetty Paërl, Jack
Botermans, and Pieter van Delft, *Shadows and Silhouettes*, offers
numerous models to follow and useful suggestions. After having
recommended a white wall or screen, the authors add:

Place the candle or the lamp on a table that is low enough (the light has to be roughly three feet from the ground). The height varies according to the height of the performer.

Place the table roughly eight feet behind the right side of the screen. The performer places himself between the lamp and the screen, his left side turned toward the source of light in such a way that the shadow is projected onto the center of the screen when he holds his hands about twenty inches from the lamp. This slightly angled position has the advantage of offering to the public a complete picture of the shadows.

AT REST

That's about all for the moment.

As one of our French Prime Ministers once said in a rather unclear fashion, "There is also an intelligence to the hand, and it isn't subject to complexes, because it communicates directly with the heart."

François Caradec

Three Wise Monkeys,
wooden carving at Tōshōgū shrine, Nikkō, Japan.

A discourse by Rodolphe Salis, as illustrated by Steinlen
(*Le Chat Noir*, October 30, 1886).

Caricature of Louis-Philippe by Charles Philipon,
printed in *Le Charivari*.

1

THE HEAD

Its reputation as the seat of intelligence naturally attracts
the presence of the hands: they scratch it.

1.01

to nod one's head vertically up and down,
back to front, one or several times
"Yes." Acquiescence.
To nod in agreement.

Renan, whom we are sure to see nodding in approval
at every antiliterary paradox that turns up, bobs his
head to signal his acquiescence.

    Goncourt, *Journal*, 1874

1.02

to gently nod one's head while turning it,
eyes shut or half-shut
"Yes." Acquiescence.
Japan.

1.03

to tip one's head back in a show of disdain
Disdain.

With a movement of the head that involves tilting it up
disdainfully, to show that we have little consideration
for someone. As sensible as the instructions we gave him
were, he did nothing but tip his head back.

    Antoine de Furetière, *Universal Dictionary*, 1690

1.04

to throw one's head back

a. "Come." A movement of the head that is a substitute for the hand gesture asking someone to come closer.

b. An arrogant manner of signaling to an inferior.

c. This movement is also a discreet way of addressing an interlocutor without being noticed.

1.05

to oscillate one's head while gently throwing it back

"Yes." A gesture of approval that can lead to confusion, so much does it resemble that of shaking the head to say "no" (see 1.09).

For a traveler to Greece, Bulgaria, as well as India and Pakistan, this is a "false friend."

1.06

to frankly shake one's head from left to right and from right to left

"No." A movement of negation and refusal. This is a widespread gesture that can be confused in Greece or in India for a gesture of assent.

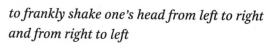

A negative was expressed by a slow movement of the head from left to right, an affirmative by a slight bend, so slight that his long hair scarcely moved.

> Jules Verne, *A Journey into the Interior of the Earth*, trans. F. Malleson, 1877

He saved a word by shaking his head, no.

> Dashiell Hammett, *The Big Knockover*

He says no with his head.
But he says yes with his heart.

> Jacques Prévert, *The Dunce*

1.07

to brusquely turn one's head to the side
"No." Negation, refusal.
A regional variant that is more frank than
the previous example.

1.08

a hesitant oscillation of one's head
from left to right and from right to left
Indecision, doubt. "Could be yes, could be no."
There is an equivalent hand gesture that
expresses the same indecision.

1.09

to abruptly throw one's head back,
eyes wide open
"No."
In the lion's share of the Arab world;
it also goes by the name of the "Greek no"
and is found in Turkey, Malta, and Sicily.

1.10

The same movement of the head can signify
"yes" in certain regional variants of northeastern
continental Africa.

1.11

to lower one's head, gazing toward the ground
A movement that can often be translated
as shame, but can also express respect,
submission, prayer.
In all cases, it involves an avoidance of looking
directly at a superior.

1.12

to pull one's hair out
This violent and degrading gesture is fortunately
a rather uncommon way to express despair.
It can also be simulated, as an act of derision.

1.13

to pull a single hair out
In Spain, children conclude a deal, an agreement,
or a pact by pulling out a single hair and blowing
on it as they cry out: "*¡Pelillos a la mar!*"

1.14

*to grab a long strand of hair between one's thumb
and index finger, pulling it above one's head*
In Spain, this gesture by a woman symbolizes
the same as pulling out one's hair, because of
either deception or frustration.

1.15

*to tousle one's hair, or pinch and scratch the top
of one's head*
Astonishment, stupefaction. Stan Laurel's
comical gesture in response to the reproaches
of his great friend Oliver Hardy.

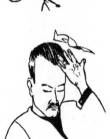

1.16

*to feign recombing one's hair discreetly with the
fingers of one hand spread apart and outstretched*
During a conversation, to ward off bad luck with
the "Hand of Fatima." Tunisia.

1.17

to scratch one's head
Perplexity. Difficulty in comprehending
a situation.

1.18

*to point one's index finger at the top of one's
head as if to indicate the spot where an idea
has just been born*
To have an idea; to be sure of oneself.
The same meaning with the finger pointed
to the temple.
Italy.

1.19

*to touch the top of one's head with the flat of
one's hand*
a. An oath. "I swear." Middle East.
b. The same gesture can be a gesture of despair
or contrition. Middle East.
c. In the Western world, it can also signify:
"How stupid I am! I never thought of that.
I nearly made a fool of myself."
d. The hand placed on top of the head was a
symbol of distress in Ancient Rome (see 1.29).

1.20

*to touch one's head with the flat of the hand, or
even to strike one's head with a closed fist*
"Knock on wood." Instead of actually touching
a piece of wood to ward off bad luck, one
derisively touches one's own head as if it were
made of wood.
Equally a sign of mockery. In Russia: "He is mad."

1.21

to swiftly pass the flat of one's hand over the top of one's head

Exasperation. "I've had it up to here, I'm fed up." Note that in the equivalent French expression, *avoir ras le bol*, in classic *argot* slang, the *bol* meant the *cul* ("the ass"), and that the origins of the expression are thus scatological and signify: "My ass is full." This original meaning is often forgotten, so much so that an occasional substitute is *ras la casquette*, or "my hat is full."

1.22

to pat one's head with the flat of the hand

A variant of the preceding example in use in South America.

1.23

to place one's hand atop one's head

Approval of a proposition; assent.

This prince, having had brought to him a chessboard, asked me through signs if I knew how to play, and if I would like to play with him. I kissed the earth; and placing my hand atop my head, I made it known that I was ready to receive this honor. [...]

    The sultan, stunned by this discourse, turned towards me, and now speaking with signs only, asked me if what his daughter had said was the truth. As I could not speak, I put my hand on my head to bear witness that the princess had spoken the truth.

> *The Thousand and One Nights*, "The Tale of the Envier and the Envied"

1.24

to hold one's hands above the head of another

This is the "laying-on of hands," the gesture performed by the bishop during the ordination ceremony of a priest.

1.25

to snap one's fingers above one's head
To affirm the truth.
England, eighteenth century.

Whilst your honour engages Mrs. Wadman in the parlour, to the right—I'll attack Mrs. Bridget in the kitchen, to the left; and having seiz'd the pass, I'll answer for it, said the corporal, snapping his fingers over his head—that the day is our own.

> Laurence Sterne, *The Life and Opinions of Tristram Shandy*, Volume VIII, chap. XXX

1.26

to strike one's skull with closed fists
A sign of mourning among some peoples.

And he began once again to strike his own forehead with one of his fists, biting his lip, and rolling towards the ceiling his wild eyes.

> Denis Diderot, *Rameau's Nephew*

1.27

to hold the nape of one's neck with both hands,
the body leaned back
A falsely laid-back posture of expectation
and superiority.
South America, most notably.

1.28

to hold both hands with fingers interlaced atop
one's head or on the nape of one's neck
Surrender. Submission. This is the gesture of the
prisoner who yields to the victor.
The same signification as two raised arms.

1.29

the hands joined and placed atop the head,
palms facing up
The sign of Masonic distress.

Sign of distress: right leg behind the left, the body slightly
leaned back, hands joined together and inverted atop
the head, palm facing out, and crying out, "To me, sons
of the Widow!"

   René Daumal

He was a Freemason, he said. As he entered into the
courtroom, he made the sign of distress, so as to appeal
to the compassion of his "brothers," if there were any in
the jury. [...]
   Was it the counsel I had given him, or his right-angled
salute that brought him his acquittal? I never knew.

   Jean Grave, *Forty Years of Anarchist Propaganda*, 1973

The same gesture in Ancient Rome, and in the
Foreign Legion: "To me, the Legion!"

1.30

both hands placed atop the head,
the body leaned forward as if about to fall
Profound despair. A gesture of oratory eloquence.

1.31

holding one's head with both hands
A theatrical gesture of despair and anxiety.

1.32

to briefly remove the hat from one's head
Greeting. The act of uncovering and displaying
one's bare head is a sign of politeness.
Hats are worn less and less, and a gesture
of the hand to touch the brim of the hat can
seem sufficient.
Young people who wear hats or baseball caps
rarely take them off; they are often intimidated
by politeness.

Boulevard types.
Engraving by Boetzel after an
illustration by Félicien Rops.

"The greeting is a form of expression, it is arrogant, simple ..."
Le Diable à Paris, Hetzel, 1845.

1.33

*to nearly place the palm of one's hand atop the
head of another as he lowers himself and is assisted
while getting into a vehicle*
Protection.
This is a gesture that an escort or a bodyguard
might make to protect the head of a dignitary
or VIP, to prevent it from possibly striking the
upper part of a low doorway.

1.34

to strike one's head with a sword or any other sharp-edged weapon held in both hands until blood is drawn

Mortification.

See also 23.84 and 31.29.

A gesture of the Shia pilgrims during Ashura, the annual commemoration of the martyrdom of Husayn, the grandson of Muhammad.

1.35

head-butt

A violent blow with the head, which is thrust into the face of one's adversary with intent to injure. A variant is a restrained and merely destabilizing head-butt, such as the one with which Zinedine Zidane struck the chest of Italian player Marco Materazzi during the World Cup of football in 2006.

2

THE TEMPLES

The temples are quite delicate.
Beneath such a thin protective covering, the fingers were
quick to discover the fragility that lay hidden.

2.01

the index finger corkscrewing against the temple,
as if to pierce through
Madness. "He's a total nutcase."

2.02

to tap against one's temple or forehead with one's
index finger
Madness. "He's crazy." The gesture can be
further accentuated by screwing the index finger
against the temple (2.01): "There's something
wrong with his head."
In the Netherlands, however, this gesture signifies
the opposite: "He's very clever."

2.03

one's thumb placed against the temple,
the hand open wide
Madness; stupidity. "He's crazy. He's an idiot."
Italy.

2.04

to make a small circular gesture around one's temple with the index finger
Madness.
In Japan, initially, the direction in which the finger turned had some importance. It seems that this subtlety is no longer taken into account. In China, the gesture signifies that the designated individual has been brainwashed or "reorganized."

A person of considerable importance in the regime, during our journey he spoke to us of this and that, and most notably about the reintegration of the Panchen Lama, who had for a time been removed from the direction of Tibetan Buddhism. And, in response to a question I asked of him, he added, while he made a small circular gesture around his right temple, "You know, he has been reorganized ..."

Marcel Mariën, *The Raft of the Memory*, 1983

2.05

one's thumb touching the temple, the fingers wiggling as if playing the piano
Madness.
Same signification as the index finger on the temple (2.02). England.

2.06

wide circular gesture of the index finger around the temple and ear
This gesture signifies that one is in the midst of considering the question: "I'm thinking about it."

With his finger, Sanscartier drew circles around his temples, as if to suggest that the operation required sober thought.

Fred Vargas, *Wash This Blood Clean from My Hand*

2.07

*hand flat, fingers tight together, palm ranging from
facing out to facing down (depending on the army),
touching the edge of one's kepi, hat, or beret*
Military salute. This is the "present arms."
There are as many varieties as there are national
armies, without getting into the creativity some
military types bring to the table when it comes
to highlighting the originality of their unit.
The military salute is given by a hat-wearing
inferior to his or her superior (who then
"returns" the salute). A soldier whose hands are
full salutes by straightening up and clicking his
heels. Civilians who have affected some sort
of military service often retain a tic, the habit
of giving a small salute (the hand touches the
man's temple, whether or not he wears a hat).
The military salute was masterfully described by
General Poilloüe de Saint-Mars, in 1893:

The military salute is open or closed.
    It is closed when one makes as if to grab the visor of
the headgear with the fingers close together, the palm of the
hand turned inward, concave, hiding about half of the
right eye, the elbow low.
    This is the salute of certain foreign armies.
    It is open when one takes the open right hand to the
right side of the visor, fingers and thumb extended and
joined together, the palm of the hand turned to the front,
broad like a flag in the wind, the elbow high.
    That is the generous and martial gesture characterized
by the open hand, the symbol of loyalty.
    That is the salute of the French army.
    The forms of this salute are very well determined by
the regulations of the internal service. One must endeavor
to thoroughly communicate them to the soldiers and to
explain to them the finer points.
    In this way, the motion of the salute must be undertaken
and released "with a lively and resolute gesture, but without
brusqueness or stiffness."
    We should not seek to teach our soldiers to abruptly
stretch out their right arm as if it were launched by a spring,

then to fold it back toward their head with a jerky motion, the forearm like the rigid wing of an aerial telegraph. It is not in our nature to be treated like automatons.

He must deploy the entire arm in a lively fashion, and yet maintain to its entirety a gracious curve by a slight bending of the elbow and the wrist, the hand open and raised as if it demanded attention. Then, straightaway that hand is returned to its regulated position by way of a second movement, which is slightly curvilinear, quick, and supple.

The military salute is a politeness to be offered; it isn't a saber thrust to be given. It is important that it appear pleasant and without violence.

The gaze which, according to regulations, must accompany the salute, must also be friendly and sincere.

When a good solider and a good officer exchange a salute, their eyes should meet one another's and at the same time exchange a flash of mutual affection. This is the sign by which one recognizes intimately disciplined troops.

2.08

the right index finger placed lightly on the temple and thrust forward

A variant of the salute, inspired by the military salute.

2.09

index and middle fingers stretched straight out, the other fingers folded back on the palm, feigning to fire a shot from a revolver into the temple by lowering the thumb, which serves as a trigger

Suicide. "It's enough to make you kill yourself."

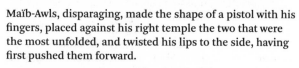

Maïb-Awls, disparaging, made the shape of a pistol with his fingers, placed against his right temple the two that were the most unfolded, and twisted his lips to the side, having first pushed them forward.

Jacques Jouet, *The Republic of Maïb-Awls*

2.10

the thumbs placed against the temples, both hands open wide, fingers spread, and the whole flapped like little wings
Mockery. Italy.
In the Middle East, this gesture can also be a way of showing "the sign of the horns."

Richard Wagner, as caricatured by André Gill
in *L'Eclipse*, 1869.

3

THE EAR

Here hides the organ responsible for hearing and
verbal communication. That doesn't stop us:
the hand still has a number of ways of touching it—
even if it means sticking a pinky finger in there.

3.01

the hand in the shape of a conch behind the ear,
enlarging the pinna in order to augment the
auditory capacity
"Louder! Speak up, I can't hear you very well."

3.02

both hands flat over the ears
A refusal to hear, the words spoken having been
so horrifying.
This is the gesture of Edvard Munch's *The Scream.*
One of the three monkeys of Chinese wisdom
covers his ears so as not to hear the noise and
temptations of the world.

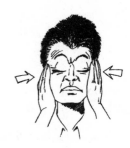

3.03

both index fingers plugging the ears
A variant of the previous example.
Refusal to hear.

3.04

fist closed next to the ear, with the exception of the thumb and the pinky, in imitation of the form of an old-fashioned telephone receiver
Telephone. A gesture that can be done from a distance and without speech, signifying: "Call me!" or "I'll call you!"

3.05

the index finger pointing toward the ear and turning as if to dial a number on an old-fashioned telephone
Telephone. As with the previous example, a gesture than can be made from a distance and without speech.
It must be remarked the extent to which certain gestures that have disappeared from contemporary life still exist in a fossilized state within gestural communication: we now only use devices with buttons, but we continue to make the gesture of turning a finger around the numbers of a dial.

3.06

one's index finger pointed into one's ear and turned quickly, while spitting out a seed or a pit, making a "prrt" sound with the lips
Children's game. Generally done at the dinner table and inviting a reprimand.

3.07

to scratch one's ear with the opposite hand passed around behind one's head
A contortion signifying that a situation is uselessly complicated. North Africa.

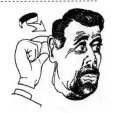

3.08

the index finger curved to scratch behind the ear
Astonishment. Perplexity.

3.09

*to touch one's ear with the fingers of the hand
clustered together*
"Be careful, someone's listening."
Mediterranean world, but also England.

3.10

*the index finger slid behind the ear to fold the
pinna forward*
Threat. "You're going to end up losing an ear."
Arab world.

3.11

the index finger gives slight taps to the earlobe
Antipathy. Russia.
Suggestion of homosexuality. Italy.

3.12

to tap the back of one's ear several times
Suggestion of homosexuality.
A similar gesture to the previous example.
Italy.

3.13

to tap one's ear with a finger
A gesture that brings luck, similar to
"knock on wood."
Turkey.

3.14

*the index finger traces a small circle around
the ear*
Threat of punishment.
Middle East.

3.15

*both hands fanned out, palms facing back,
both pinkies stuck into the ears*
The Arab way of making horns to designate
a cuckold.

3.16

*both thumbs in the ears, hands open, palms to the
front, which are waved back and forth*
A child's teasing; the tongue is often stuck out at
the same time.

3.17

*the thumb stuck into an ear, the open hand waving
back and forth*
A child's teasing. A variant of the previous
example.

3.18

*the thumb in one ear, the open hand waving back
and forth*
Poverty. Embarrassment. "I'm broke."
Portugal.

3.19

*to hold one's earlobe between the thumb
and index finger*
Disappointment. A gesture that might indicate
that the person you were speaking with has
taken off without paying, and has left you to take
care of the check.
Spain; also noted in England.

3.20

*to pull on one's earlobe with the thumb and
index finger*
Threat: "You had better watch out."
Greece and Turkey.

3.21

to hold and gently wiggle the earlobe
Pleasure. An exquisite flavor. "It's delicious."
Portugal. Brazil.

3.22

to pull on both earlobes simultaneously
Remorse. The gesture of an inferior who has just
been reprimanded and who apologizes.
India.

Albrecht Dürer,
Self-Portrait with a Bandage.

4

THE FOREHEAD

"To meet something head on":
this expression underscores the role of this part of
the face as that which contains the seat of intelligence.
But the forehead doesn't only conceal the mind ...

4.01

to pass one's thumb across the width of the
forehead as if to wipe away beads of sweat
Fatigue. Weariness. Boredom.
Noted in Naples as early as 1832 by Andrea
de Jorio.

4.02

to pass the back of one's hand across the forehead
Feeling faint. "I don't feel well, I think I'm going
to faint." A melodramatic gesture that is often
used in mockery.

4.03

to rub one's forehead with a closed fist
There's a screw loose in his head, he's crazy.
Native Americans.

4.04

to grasp one's forehead with both hands
Profound despondency.

4.05

the palm of the hand placed on one's forehead
Despondency.

4.06

the hand in the shape of a visor in front of or above the forehead
To look far into the distance;
trying to see something that is moving away.

4.07

to pass one's hand in the shape of a visor in front of the forehead, and to shake it, as if to shake away sweat
Signifies that one has been afraid, that one has had a narrow escape.

4.08

to pass one's hand before the face and the forehead as if to chase away a fly
Madness. "He's lost his mind."
Most notably the Netherlands.

4.09

to quickly pass one's hand in front of the forehead
Exasperation. Weariness.
A variant of 1.21.

4.10

*to brush the tips of the fingers against the forehead,
then the chest, then again the forehead*
Arab greeting. "I offer you my spirit, my heart,
my mind."

4.11

*to brush the tips of the fingers against the forehead
while the head is bent forward*
A simplified version of the previous greeting.
Very common in the Arab world.

4.12

*the index and middle fingers successively touch
one's forehead, sternum, left shoulder, and
right shoulder*
Sign of the Cross.
This gesture can be more restrained and limited
to the four points of the chest.

4.13

*to slap one's forehead with the palm of the hand,
hard enough to make a noise*
Self-criticism. "How stupid of me!"

4.14

to strike one's forehead with the back of the hand
A variant of the previous example.
Middle East.

4.15

to tap one's forehead with the index finger
a. Madness

Eliasar watched him while shaking his head, then turned toward Captain Heresa, and, striking his forehead with a finger, he raised his eyes toward the ceiling of the room.

Pierre Mac Orlan, *The Song of the Crew*

b. This gesture can have a positive signification: "There's something going on in there," or more simply, "I have an idea."

4.16

to tap one's forehead with the fingertips of one hand
A variant of the previous example.
Mediterranean region.

4.17

to tap one's forehead with the fingertips of both hands
Exaggerated variant of the preceding examples.
Mediterranean region.

4.18

to tap one's forehead with the index finger, not far from the temple
Intelligence. "He is smart," or, "I understand."

4.19

to touch the ground with one's forehead during kneeling prostration
See 36.04. Islam.

5

THE EYEBROWS
AND THE EYELASHES

*The hairs of the upper face, which we pluck but—
unlike those of the chin—do not shave, have found, thanks
to their mobility, their uses in facial expression
and the communication of feelings.*

5.01

to raise one's eyebrows

a. Astonishment, concern.

b. Can also be a sign of complicity or a greeting
exchanged from afar; even a signal of seduction.

5.02

to raise a single eyebrow

Concern, skepticism.

5.03

to furrow one's brow

a. Threat; concern. The furrowed brows are
one of the first threatening gestures made by an
adult to a child.

b. This can also be a gesture of denial or refusal.

c. Can also sometimes be a sign of connivance.

5.04

*the thumb and the index finger pinch the arch of
the eyebrows*

Madness. "You're crazy." Italy.

5.05

*to touch the middle of the arch of the eyebrows
with the index finger*
Signifies guilt at not having been able to act in
a certain situation.
Arab world.

5.06

*to smooth a brow with the little finger, having
moistened it with the tongue*
Exaggerated vanity or flirtation.
Suggestion of homosexuality.

5.07

to flutter or bat one's eyelashes
A sign of complicity similar to the wink of an eye.
Seduction.

6

THE EYE

Protected by the eyebrows and the eyelashes, the eye is the organ of sight. And with that eye-opening statement, we're well on our way! Feast your eyes on these many examples, because it seems our eyes were bigger than our stomachs.

6.01

to peek through the slightly spread fingers of the hand
Curiosity.

Illustration by
Jean Veber.

6.02

the index finger placed on the lower eyelid, pulling it downward
This gesture has several meanings:
a. The most common meaning in Europe is to signify disbelief or skepticism: *Mon oeil* ("my eye") for the French is similar to "My foot" in English.
b. But it can also signify "Be careful, I'm watching you. Watch it!" in Europe and North Africa.
c. In Italy, this gesture signifies that the person being discussed is shrewd, crafty, and that one must be cautious of him or her.
d. It can also mean that a beautiful girl has caught one's eye.

6.03

to rub the upper eyelid with the tip of the index finger
A gesture of protection against the Evil Eye. Middle East.

6.04

to touch the index finger to the lower eyelid of the eye situated on the same side as the hand
Stupidity. "I see you have made a fool of yourself." Arab world.

6.05

to place the index finger on the upper eyelid of the eye situated on the same side as the hand
Oath. "I swear it on my eye."
Arab world.

6.06

to touch a finger to one's eye
A kind of warning, since "sticking a finger in your own eye" in France is similar to the Anglophone expression "You're kidding yourself," or stronger yet, "You don't know your ass from your elbow."

6.07

eyes wide open, eyebrows furrowed
Flirtatious look: "I'm interested."

6.08

ferocious look, eyebrows furrowed
The manner of amiably welcoming invited guests in Melanesia, according to Otto Klineberg.

6.09

eyes wide open beneath furrowed brows, gazing fixedly at one's interlocutor
A silent threat generally made by an adult to a child. This is "the stern look."

6.10

to roll one's eyes back or to the side in such a way as to show only the whites
According to Alfred Delvau (1867), this gesture is related to French argot, and known as "giving the carp eye," which is an amorous invitation.

6.11

to raise one's eyes skyward
Exasperation, disbelief. "That's nonsense!"

6.12

eyes closed, the mouth making a face of disgust
Exaggerated disgust.

6.13

to make a circle with the thumbs and index fingers of both hands, placing them over one's eyes
To photograph. To look.
In a famous photograph, Pope John Paul II teasingly "photographs" the photographers taking pictures of him. It's a gesture of irritation.

6.14

to look through both fists, which are stacked one atop the other to form a telescope
A gesture by the watcher means to draw the attention of the person being watched.
Most notably Brazil.

6.15

to pass one's hand before the eyes, moving from above to below
Poor vision. "You're blind. Pay closer attention."
Italy.

6.16

to place the index and middle fingers atop one's closed eyes
Oath. "I swear it upon my eyes. Strike me blind if I'm lying."
Netherlands.

6.17

to place both hands over one's eyes in order not to see
A gesture of modesty and shame.
This is also one of the three gestures of the monkeys of Chinese wisdom: the sage prefers not to see.

6.18

rubbing one's eyes with closed fists
Feigning to awaken from slumber, from a state of sleepiness.

... a rub of the eyelids with the most diligent knuckles and phalanges.

> Carlo Emilio Gadda, *That Awful Mess on the Via Merulana*, trans. William Weaver, 1965

6.19

to rub one's eye with one's fist
Indifference. "I didn't even blink an eye; what you say doesn't interest me."

6.20

sidelong look, head tilted away
This is a flirtatious look that is hidden behind
a false showing of humility.

6.21

to bat one's eyelids
A prelude to the exchange of flirtatious looks.

He then made a series of signs to Mésange, with eye and
hand. Mésange understood admirably (but what is not
possible to communicate by gestures? what a superfluous
luxury is the use of the vocal cords!—such were the heights
to which Pierrot's thought then rose).
   Raymond Queneau, *Pierrot Mon Ami*,
   trans. Barbara Wright, 1987

6.22

to wink an eye at one's interlocutor
A wink of complicity.
The wink can be considered vulgar;
it is an unmistakable invitation.

It is a great impoliteness to gaze upon a person while holding
one eye closed as would a crossbowman who is aiming
at a target, & it is not of the least rusticity to look over one's
shoulder by turning the head, which is a sign of contempt.
   The Rules of Puerile and Respectable Civility, Troyes,
   early eighteenth century

6.23

*to pass the back of the index finger across the rim
of one's eyelid, as if wiping away a tear*
Sadness. Feigned regret.

6.24

the forearm bent back to cover one's eyes
Feigning to hide one's tears. Sadness that can be
genuine to a greater or lesser extent.

6.25

shedding tears

Some people can shed tears at will. By doing so they express a sadness of varying sincerity.

Coming to the weeping itself, cover the face decorously, using both hands, palms inward. Children are to cry with the sleeve of the dress or shirt pressed against the face, preferably in a corner of the room. Average duration of the cry, three minutes.

> Julio Cortázar, "Instructions on How to Cry," *Cronopios and Famas*, trans. Paul Blackburn, 1969

6.26

to look one's interlocutor up and down after donning a monocle

Superiority.

A fossilized gesture, now that men no longer wear monocles.

7

THE NOSE

One may wonder what sort of "gestures" can be carried out with the organ of smell. And yet here we've sniffed out over forty of them!

7.01

to raise one's nose in the direction of the speaker
Superiority. Contempt. Mockery.

7.02

to push up one's nose with one's index finger
Refusal addressed to an inferior.
Central Europe.

7.03

to twist one's nose to the side
Slight movement indicating displeasure, disgust.

7.04

to wrinkle one's nose
Disgust; sense of smell offended by an unpleasant odor.

7.05

to move one's nose to the side
Denial, less frank than shaking one's head (1.06).

7.06

to touch one's nose with the tip of one's index finger,
perpendicularly to one's face
Self. Identity.
Japan.

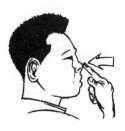

7.07

same gesture, but pointing one's index finger to
one's nose from the front
Self. Identity.
China. (In the East, one speaks of the self
by designating the nose, whereas in the West,
one touches one's chest.)

7.08

to press one's index finger against one's nose
Racist insult addressed to a black man or woman
whose nose is larger than that of the Arab. This
gesture can also convey a threat to crush the
adversary's nose.
Arab world.

7.09

to touch the tip of one's nose
Oath. "I swear it on my nose."
Arab world.

7.10

to stroke one's nose from root to tip
Avarice. Indicates that the person with whom
one is speaking is miserly.
The Netherlands.

7.11

to rub the ala of one's nose
Indicates that one disagrees with the person
with whom one is speaking.
Greece.

7.12

to give the tip of one's nose a little tap
Insult. Suggestion of homosexuality.
Middle East.

7.13

to pat one's nose
This gesture has numerous meanings:
a. In England, it can mean that one is sharing
a secret. But it is also a threat directed to anyone
who is getting involved in something that
doesn't concern them.
b. In the south of Italy, when it is a question
of someone clever: "He knows how to figure
things out."
c. Again in Italy, it is a warning:
"Don't trust him."
d. In England and Italy, it is also a sign
of complicity.
e. Elsewhere, it is a threat: "I know what
you're after"; or a warning: "Don't trust him."

7.14

to tap the ala of one's nose with one's index finger while looking straight at one's interlocutor
a. In England and Scotland, but also in southern Italy, this gesture means that a secret is being shared.
b. In France, it is a gesture of complicity and agreement.
c. But for a Welshman or a Frenchman, it means: "He's a snitch, he's nosy."

7.15

to slide one's index finger or one's hand under one's nose, above the upper lip
Disappointment. Indicates that it is too late; that one missed something; that it slipped out from right under one's nose.

And he passed his hand horizontally under his nose, tracing waves like an immaterial odor or a pan-fried sole on the lam.
  Jacques Jouet, *The Republic of Maïb-Awls*

7.16

to tap one's nostrils from bottom to top with one's index finger
Bad smell. "That stinks," in the literal sense and the figurative.

7.17

to sniff while sliding one's index finger horizontally under one's nose
Drugs. Allusion to cocaine: the gesture indicates that one wants some or that one is selling some.

7.18

to pinch one's nostrils and rub the bridge of the nose from bottom to top
Admiration. This gesture designates an intelligent person (who puts his glasses back into place by sliding them up his nose).
Italy.

7.19

to place the palm of one's hand on the interlocutor's nose and face, then lower it, rubbing from top to bottom
This is a means of rejecting, teasing, or cursing in a joking manner.
North Africa.

7.20

to cover one's face with the palm of one's hand, fingers extended, set at the center of one's nose
Shame. To hide the face so that the redness of one's shame can't be seen.

7.21

to grasp one's nose with a hooked index finger, fist clenched
Distrust. "If I do it, it will be in spite of myself."
Arab world.

7.22

to grab one's nose with a clenched fist and twist it
Indicates that the person with whom one is speaking is inebriated. "This guy's completely sloshed."
A typically French gesture.

7.23

to grab one's nose in one's fist
(without squeezing too tightly) and twisting it
Obscene gesture. The closed fist represents the
anus. The gesture suggests that the designated
person is a kiss-ass who wouldn't hesitate to
stick his nose into your anus.
North America.

7.24

to encircle one's nose with one's thumb and
index finger forming a ring, and to turn them
(in either direction)
Obscene gesture. The designated person is
a homosexual.
North America.

7.25

to pass the index and middle fingers, both
extended, from top to bottom along the entire
length of one's nose
Lack of money. "I'm broke."
Spain. Portugal.

7.26

to pick one's nose with the index finger
Insult.
Variant: thumb and index finger in the two
nostrils. The gesture can be amplified by flicking
the fingers, once they have emerged from the
nose, in the direction of the person being insulted.
Middle East.

7.27

with one's index finger pointing to either side of one's
nose, to turn the former as if to pierce the latter
Defiance. "You won't make me do what I don't
want to do."
Greece.

7.28

to squeeze one's nostrils between the thumb and
index finger
Bad smell. "That stinks," in the literal sense
and the figurative.
In England, one completes the gesture by pulling
on an imaginary toilet chain with the other hand.

7.29

to pinch the tip of one's nose between the thumb
and index finger and pull on it
Threat. "You'll get yours."
South America.

7.30

to pinch one's nose and stick out one's tongue at the
same time while emitting a "blech!"
Disgust. "You're disgusting ..."
Gesture made by children and adolescents.

7.31

to set one's index and middle fingers on one's nostrils
Facility.
Similar meaning to the Anglophone expression
"With one hand tied behind my back." Or, as the
French expression describes it, doing something
"with one's fingers in one's nose."
France.

7.32

to pinch one's nose with one's index and middle fingers, pulling it from right to left
Distrust. "There's something rotten here, I don't trust it."
Italy.

7.33

to take one's nose between one's index and middle fingers
Intelligence. "He's a clever one."
Already noticed in Naples by Andrea de Jorio in 1832.
Italy.

7.34

with the index and middle fingers in the shape of a V, to put one's palm against one's face, nose in the point of the V
Obscene gesture, the V representing the female genitals and the nose the penis.
Arab world. South America.

7.35

to pretend to grab the nose of a playmate, represented by holding one's thumb between one's folded-down index and middle fingers
Children's game. "I've got your nose!"

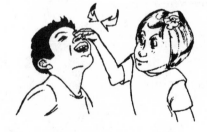

7.36

hand open with fingers fanned out, thumb set
on the tip of one's nose; one can also move the
hand about
Mockery. To thumb one's nose. To "cock a snook"
[UK—Trans.]. In England, allusion to a fan.
In Germany, it's known as making a long nose,
"die lange Nase."

7.36b

same gesture with both hands, one extending
the other, the thumb of the second hand resting
against the little finger of the first
This derisive gesture is very old and very
widespread. It can be found on an engraving
by Pieter Bruegel the Elder, *The Feast of Fools.*
A related gesture, thumb set on one's mouth
and not on the nose, is mockery on the part of
the Jews jeering at Christ, as depicted in two
altarpieces by Hans Holbein.

Advertisement, 1900s.

7.37

to press the back of one's hand against one's nose while nodding one's head
Greeting. Friendly gesture toward someone too far away to be able to rub faces with.
Arab world.

7.38

to rub one's nose against that of one's interlocutor, or against his or her cheek
Friendly greeting.
Less common than the kiss on the cheek, the embrace, or the handshake, the rubbing of noses is still done in Polynesia, Malaysia, and among the Inuit.

7.39

to quickly rub the end of one another's nose three times while smacking one's lips
Friendly greeting among the Bedouin tribes.
Arab world.

7.40

to set one's lips on the nose of the interlocutor
from whom one wishes to obtain forgiveness,
for example after a minor argument
Friendly greeting.
Arab world.

7.41

to give a little tap under one's nose with the
index finger, while tilting one's head back slightly
and raising one's eyebrows
Accusation of snobbery and pretentiousness.
"To stick one's nose up," which in German is
"*die Nase hoch tragen.*"

7.42

to point one's index finger at the chest of one's
interlocutor to indicate an imaginary stain,
and, as he lowers his head to look at it, to pull
up his nose with the same index finger
Mockery. Children's game.

7.43

gesture of the nostril

Most of all, I remember a charming gesture you make with
your nostril when, lying next to me, you turn over on your
side to look at me.

    Gustave Flaubert, *Correspondence*, 1846

Door to the house of Salvator Rosa, Rome.
Photo by Paul McCoubrie (full credit on p. 317).

8

THE MOUTH

We might believe that the seat of speech (without considering ventriloquists and flatulists) has no need for the assistance of hand gestures when it comes to expressing emotions and sensations. Numerous adjectives confirm this to be true: *foul*, *open*, *loud*, *smart*, *foaming*, *pouty*, *watering*—the mouth can be all of these things and many more still.

Whereas in English, *to have your heart in your mouth* means to be very nervous, in French, it is inverted and has a different meaning. As Raymond Queneau puts it in *Loin de Rueil*: "He coldly left like in a transitional scene, just like that, in the night, mouth in heart, without a word." Typically, in French, this means to put on airs or to simper.

The French also have the expression *la bouche en cul de poule*, which literally means "to have a chicken's ass for a mouth," but idiomatically indicates that someone has put on a honeyed or fawning look, puckering his lips or not, in the hopes of getting what he wants. The mouth can be mysterious and arouse fantasies, which Simone de Beauvoir acknowledged in her book *Memoirs of a Dutiful Daughter*:

I would have very much liked to find out through what mechanism it was that the contact of two mouths brought about sensual pleasure: often, looking at the lips of a young man or a young woman, I was amazed.

The mouth also knows how to keep quiet: it is upon the mouth that the monkey of Chinese wisdom places its hands to signify that silence is always worth more than an imprudent word.

8.01

to touch the index finger to one's lips
Silence. Do not make noise; be quiet.
In the Arab world, one blows on the finger.

Then recommending me, by an impressive gesture,
to keep silence, he went into the boat which awaited him.

> Jules Verne, *A Journey into the Interior of the Earth*,
> trans. F. Malleson, 1877

8.02

*to bring two or three fingers, pinched together,
to the mouth several times*
Hunger. This is the most widespread sign of
hunger, used to ask for food to eat.

8.03

*to bring one's hand to one's mouth in the shape of
a small vessel, the thumb and index finger touching
in a circle, the whole in imitation of a cup from
which to drink*
Thirst. "I need something to drink! I'm thirsty!"

8.04

*to bring one's hand toward one's mouth as if to
hold in one's speech*
Indignation; surprise. A gesture of eloquence.

8.05

*to bring one's hand toward one's mouth without
quite touching it*
Modesty. A gesture of eloquence employed by
the great orators of antiquity.

8.06

to bring one's fist to one's mouth
A regional variant of the previous example.
Arab world, but has equally been adopted in
monasteries.

8.07

to raise a half-closed fist with the pinky jutting out
to the front, the thumb turned toward the mouth,
head tipped back
Thirst. A gesture that signifies drinking straight
from a bottle or wineskin: "Bring me something
to drink! I'm thirsty!"
Mediterranean world.

8.08

to feign putting one's lips to a trumpet formed by
the closed fist, thumb turned toward the mouth,
little finger stuck out to the front
Trumpet. Children's game. But also mockery
with regard to a pretentious individual.

8.09

to insert the index finger into the mouth and use
it to make the cheek "pop"
To make a face.
Mockery. "Panurge bobbed and made mouths at
him in token of derision" (Rabelais, *The Works of*
Rabelais, Book IV, trans. Motteux, 1708).
Called *la babou* in French, named for a witch
with great big lips.

8.10

*to open one's mouth, raise one's eyebrows,
and widen one's eyes*
Astonishment.
A universal expression, according to Darwin,
in *The Expression of the Emotions in Man and
Animals*, 1872.

8.11

to smile
The smile, like laughter, is unique to humankind.
It isn't always involuntary, but is quite often
forced. This is what we might refer to as "the
salesman's smile," or the carnivorous smile of
the politician on the campaign trail.
According to Klineberg, the smile in Melanesia
expresses sadness. In Asia, it is wiped away the
moment the interlocutor becomes interested in
the conversation.

8.12

*to inflate the lower jaw area while pushing one's
tongue out from between the teeth and lips,
at the same time as scratching one's armpits*
Mockery. A gesture imitating the monkey
scratching itself.

Maïb-Awls inflated the lower part of his mouth and wedged
his tongue between his lower jaw and the skin, scratching
his armpits at the same time.

Jacques Jouet, *The Republic of Maïb-Awls*

8.13

the hand forming a cone before the mouth
To whisper a secret; to call quietly to someone.

8.14

*the right hand, with all five fingers gathered together, is touched to one's mouth, the lips puckered (*en cul de poule, *see above), and then partially opened while the hand abruptly pulls away with a "pschitt!" of pleasure*
Exquisite, delicious.
Italy.

8.15

the hand open, pinching the edge of the lips between the thumb and index finger, only to pull them away abruptly
A variant of the previous example.
Exquisite, delicious. A gesture to be made after having tasted a dish.

8.16

the hand in front of the mouth, fingers slightly spread, palm facing out
Confusion; shyness.
A gesture common among young girls in North America.

8.17

the hand in front of the mouth, palm turned toward the face
A variant of the previous example.
Enthusiasm. "How adorable!" ("The Behaviors of Paris," mimed French chanson from the eighteenth century.)

8.18

to thrust one's thumb into the mouth, inflate the cheeks, and blow
Indifference. Defiance, disregard for danger.
The Netherlands.

8.19

to suck the tip of one's thumb
Immaturity. Mockery directed to an interlocutor that suggests he has remained a child and still sucks his thumb.
In the Netherlands, this gesture can also signify that one's interlocutor is a liar.

8.20

the hand folded as if it is holding something (food) with the fingertips, brought quickly to the mouth
Hunger.

8.21

to place the tip of one's index finger on the lips while lowering one's eyes
Contrition. Regret.

8.22

to insert one's middle finger into one's mouth through pinched lips, then to remove it and hold it up for an interlocutor
Obscene gesture. Threat of sodomy. Insult.

8.23

*to place one's index finger in one's mouth and
to quickly suck at it*
Misery. Lack of money.
Arab world.

8.24

*to touch one's lips with the tips of the thumb, index,
and middle fingers, then to touch them to one's
forehead while slightly tilting the head*
"Salaam!" A simplified version of the Arab
greeting, which is accompanied by the words
"Salaam alaikum" (Peace be upon you).

8.25

to kiss the tip of one's index finger
To kiss from afar. A kiss farewell.

Suddenly, Mlle. de Cardoville laid her finger upon her lips,
blew a couple of kisses in the direction towards which she
had been looking, and all at once disappeared.

    Eugène Sue, *The Wandering Jew*, trans. anon., 1889

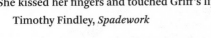

In another variant, the kiss is then placed on the
lips of the loved one.

She kissed her fingers and touched Griff's lips.

    Timothy Findley, *Spadework*

Blowing a kiss.
Illustration by Fernand Fau.

8.26

lightly holding a woman's right hand,
the man bends down and feigns placing a kiss
on the joints of her fingers
Gallantry.
This gesture is the kiss of the hand. It must be
executed without a sound from the lips, lightly,
and rather quickly. This homage meets the rules
of international etiquette. It can also be used
on the hand of a sovereign or a high-ranking
religious dignitary.

> She ... held out to him her fingers with their pale nails,
> the back of her hand facing up. Simon was not in the habit
> of kissing hands. He lifted her wrist belatedly. A faint smile,
> the first she had worn since the beginning of the interview,
> appeared on the lips of Mme Eterlin.
>
> Maurice Druon, *The Great Families*, 1948

These days, this gesture has become a sign of
affectation, sullied by ridicule. The usage
of this gesture by the French, well on its way
to disappearing, has been the cause of much
laughter by Americans. This is corroborated
by a photograph of President Jacques Chirac
kissing the hand of Condoleezza Rice
(see page 11).

to kiss another's hand while giving a slight bow
This variation is a sign of profound respect. This
gesture seems currently to be reserved for use
by the subjects of the King of Morocco, but it
adapts very well to use with any other sitting
monarch or dictator.
It is equally a sign of respect for the Queen
of England.

8.27

to brush one's lips with one's fingertips, then move the hand away from the mouth as if to throw the kiss to the person it is intended for
Admiration.
A gesture known to the Greeks and Romans of antiquity: back then it was a gesture of adoration offered to a deity.
Used in Europe, with the exception of the Anglo-Saxon countries.

8.28

to place a kiss on one's fingertips and, with the hand flat and palm up, to blow the kiss in the direction of the man or woman to whom it is being sent
Admiration. To blow someone a kiss.

Maïb-Awls placed his right hand upon his heart, removed it, placed it horizontally in front of his mouth, fingers directed at Brout', and blew.

Jacques Jouet, *The Republic of Maïb-Awls*

8.29

to kiss one's hand while looking at a loved one
Long-distance kiss. Admiration. Adoration.

8.30

to place a kiss on the palm of one's hand, held vertically against the face, then to hold it out toward a loved one
Admiration. Adoration.

8.31

*to kiss the knuckles of the back of one's own hand,
then to turn the palm skyward while raising the
eyes to the heavens*
Worship, adoration. Prayer of gratitude.
Arab world.

8.32

to quickly cover one's mouth with one's hand
a. A blunder. "That just slipped out." Placing
one's hand over one's mouth prevents one from
saying anything further.
b. Politeness. "When you cough, cover your
mouth with your hand," we often tell children.

8.33

both hands covering one's mouth
Confusion. Dismay.

8.34

*to join the fingertips of both hands together,
placing the tips of the index fingers on the lips*
Thought, reflection.

8.35

*both hands cupped slightly to form a megaphone
that surrounds the mouth on both sides*
A useful gesture that accompanies a call of
the voice.

8.36

*to blow the smoke from a cigarette in the direction
of a person whom one desires*
Flirtation. Amorous invitation.
Middle East.

8.37

*to kiss the forehead of a superior; or the hand;
or the foot*
Respect.
Arab world.
The kiss of the young gangster on the fist
of his Mafia godfather is a variant of this
Mediterranean gesture.

8.38

*with fingers spread, to wave one's hand in front
of one's mouth as if to fan it*
A way of indicating that a dish is too hot or
too spicy and is burning one's mouth.

8.39

*both index fingers in the mouth, pulling its corners
horizontally away from each other*
One of the typical funny faces made by children.
In 1971, American psychologist Paul Ekman
distinguished seven primary meanings for the
facial expressions: happiness, anger, surprise,
sadness, disgust, contempt, and fear. Their
manifestation is linked to the innervation of
certain facial muscles. To these involuntary
grimaces and facial expressions we must add
those made voluntarily by children to mock
or ridicule.

8.40

to feign as if to spit on the ground
An insult directed at an interlocutor,
profound contempt.
Mediterranean world.

8.41

to whistle
While whistling isn't a gesture, strictly speaking,
neither is it an articulated language.
We could classify here whistling addressed to a
person at whom we are jeering, appreciative
whistling aimed at a passing woman, a sudden
whistle to call a person or animal (such as a dog)
or intended as a signal, the whistle of a traffic
controller, etc., with or without the aid of fingers.

8.42

to feign a yawn, hand in front of one's mouth
Boredom. "He is so boring with his long-winded
speeches!"

9

THE LIPS

It takes two of them to shut one's mouth.

9.01
for a woman to touch her upper lip with a finger
Homosexuality.

9.02
to twirl an imaginary mustache by pinching it
between the thumb and index finger
A gesture that indicates swagger, bravado; but
also mockery of an individual's pretentiousness.

9.03
to squeeze one's lips between the thumb and index
finger so as to close one's mouth
Silence. "My lips are sealed."

9.04
to quickly pass the thumb along one's upper lip as
if closing a zipper
Secret. Silence. "I won't say a thing, it's a secret."

9.05

to place one's index finger perpendicular to one's upper lip and hold it in place for a moment
Silence.

As he was about to open his mouth to ask her something, she gently placed her right hand against his lips, placing on her own a finger from her left. Don't say a word, she said softly, it's too soon, it could end up hurting you.

Jean Echenoz, *Piano*

9.06

to place one's index finger against one's lower lip
This gesture signifies a desire to taste a dish, a sweet. The same gesture can signify a desire to speak, which can lead to misunderstandings. Greece and the Mediterranean world.

9.07

to lower the corners of one's lips
Disbelief. Disappointment.
This is to pout, lowering the lips and squeezing
them together.

9.08

the index or the middle finger hooked over the
lower lip or the teeth
Shyness. Perplexity.

9.09

to make a motion with the lips as if to kiss
Another way to blow a kiss (England), similar to
blowing a kiss from the fingertips.

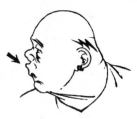

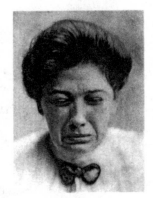

Postcards from the Universal Postal Union.

9.10

a kiss on the cheek
This token of affection has taken over in Europe
over the past decades as a greeting between a
man and a woman, and signifies nothing more
than a handshake between two men. It is the
man who gives the *baiser* (kiss) to the woman
(and not the inverse), with one single kiss
in England (if one dares!), two (both cheeks) in
the larger part of Europe, three in Belgium and
in France (and between Freemasons), even four
sometimes in Paris ... but never in Japan.
Women have begun to complain about the
contact with unshaven cheeks.
Over the past fifteen years, men have
increasingly taken to the kiss in greeting instead
of the shaking of hands, a trend that seems
to have been imported to France by North
Americans.

9.11

*contact of the lips (and of the tongue) with
those of a partner*
Love.
Oral kissing that can become lingual,
depending on the fancy and imagination
of the amorous parties.
Kissing on the mouth in public is not permitted
in some places. It can be considered vulgar,
even obscene. In the West, kisses are often
exchanged in the streets (see, for example, the
photo by Robert Doisneau, *The Kiss by the
Hôtel-de-Ville*).

Their kiss is endless. Chrysis would seem to have under her tongue, not milk and honey, as in Holy writ, but living, mobile, enchanted water. And this multiform tongue itself, now incurved like an arch, now rolled up like a spiral, now shrinking into its hiding-place, now darting forth like a flame, more caressing than the hand, more expressive than the eyes, circling, flower-like, into a pistil, or thinning away into a petal, this ribbon of flesh that hardens when it quivers and softens when it licks, Chrysis animates it with all the resources of her endearing and passionate fantasy.

> Pierre Louÿs, *Ancient Manners, or Aphrodite*,
> Carrington translation, 1906

In Russia, men may share a kiss on the mouth as a simple greeting. In 1968, during the "Prague Spring," Alexander Dubček, First Secretary of the Communist Party of Czechoslovakia, irritated by Leonid Brezhnev's ardent kisses, took up the habit of carrying a large bouquet of flowers in his arms, which spared him the aggression of his Soviet master.

9.12
to kiss one's crossed index fingers
An oath on the Cross.
Italy. Christian Mediterranean regions.

9.13
to smack one's tongue, briefly and loudly, against the corners of one's lips
Acquiescence. Yes. All right.
Considered vulgar.

Muriel Cooper, Director of Design at the MIT Press from 1967 to 1974,
then Special Projects Director; founder of the Visible Language Workshop,
later a component of the MIT Media Lab, where she taught as a professor
until her death in 1994. Photo from 1988. Courtesy MIT Museum.

10

THE TONGUE

The organ of taste, this little lump of mobile flesh intervenes more than you would think in human relations—amorous relations, of course (see the lips), but also in several others that may not immediately come to mind. Not to mention for speech, when it is necessary: each people has its own tongue, and they make sure not to let the cat anywhere near it.

10.01

to frankly stick one's tongue out to one's interlocutor
Sign of contempt and provocation. It has precisely the same meaning among "poorly raised" children as the word "shit" does among adults. It can be embellished by adding both hands, open, with the thumbs stuck in the ears, waved quickly or slowly as the case may be. But adults use this gesture as well. We're all familiar with the famous photo of Albert Einstein, sticking his tongue out at one of his photographers.
To stick out one's tongue can also signify "Hello" in the Tibetan fashion.

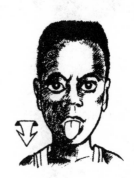

10.02

to stick out one's tongue while making a hand gesture that mimics throwing something in front of oneself
Insult. This is the previous gesture, compounded by a movement of reject.
Africa.

10.03

to stick one's tongue out through slightly open lips, and to move it in and out several times
Erotic invitation.
"It's a conventional signal that has been taken up by the *tribades*," said Léo Taxil in *Fin-de-Siècle Corruption* (1891), writing on the subject of women soliciting other women in the Bois de Boulogne and along the Champs-Elysées.

10.04

to stick one's tongue out with a look of concentration
Mockery. A way of teasing someone who claims to have a lot of work to do, tongue hanging out from exhaustion.

10.05

to quickly stick one's tongue out, touching it with a bent index finger
Chatter, idle talk. "Listen to her prattling on."
South America.

10.06

to touch the tip of the tongue with the tip of the index finger, which is then touched to the nose
Haste. "Hurry up."
Arab world.

10.07
to pass the tongue between the lips, sliding it from one corner of the lips to the other
Obscene gesture. Erotic invitation.

Quietly, her fists against her hips, she had stopped in front of them. For a moment, they hesitated. From the way that she passed her tongue between her lips, they understood her aim to reward the victor. This was her only gesture.

Charles-Henry Hirsch, *The Tiger and the Poppy*, 1905

10.08
to stick the tip of the tongue out, bringing it immediately back in
Awkwardness. The feeling of having said too much.
China.

10.09
to moisten the thumb with the tongue, then move the hands to the waist, swaying forward and back
Obscene gesture.
Lebanon.

10.10
to slowly pass the tongue across the lips;
to lick one's lips
Expectation of a gustatory pleasure.
The same movement of the tongue can also be obscene (erotic invitation).

10.11

to run the tongue across the fingers of one's hand
To enjoy the flavor of a dish or a sweet.
"To lick one's fingers" with satisfaction. Or even better: "To lick one's fingers all the way up to the elbow."

10.12

to open the mouth just far enough to allow someone to see the rolled tongue between one's lips
Obscene gesture.
Erotic invitation.

10.13

to emit a whistling noise with one's tongue between one's teeth
Indifference.

The boy placed his tongue between his teeth and let them hear a faint hiss of indifference.
   "I don't know," he said elegantly.

   Villiers de l'Isle-Adam, *Tribulat Bonhomet*

11

THE TEETH

While listening to your internal organs with a stethoscope,
French doctors used to ask you to repeat "33, 33 ..." (trente-trois).
Dentists were happy enough with "32."

11.01

to grit one's teeth
Vigor. Resistance. To encourage renewed effort.

11.02

to nibble on one's lower lip while shaking
one's head
Exasperation. To hold in rage.

11.03

to bite the index finger on the knuckle that lies
between the second and third phalanx
Regret. Misfortune. Frustration. "Well, that was
a real kick in the teeth."
This gesture can also be a sign of anger.

11.04

to bite one's index finger, then shake it
Admiration. Luck. "Hot damn! What a lucky
duck!"

11.05

to bite one's thumb

a. Provocation.

Sampson's "I will take the wall of any man ..." or Abram's "Do you bite your thumb at us, sir?" were the legal tender of the troublemaker, around 1592, in Shakespeare's fraudulent Verona and in the beer halls, brothels, and bear-baiting pits of London.

> Jorge Luis Borges, *History of Eternity*, trans. Allen, Levine, and Weinberger, 1999

b. It is also, in Syria, a way in which a boy can show how much being rebuffed by a girl he loves has made him suffer.

11.06

to bite both thumbs, directing the hands toward one's interlocutor, fingers spread.
Surrender. "I give up."
Was at one point in use among the Bedouin tribes.
Arab world.

11.07

to bite the nail of the index finger
Astonishment.

... the old man, wide-eyed with astonishment, chewed on the nail of his left index finger.

> Sadegh Hedayat, *The Blind Owl*

This is the classic gesture to express surprise. It is often found on ancient miniatures.
Middle East.

11.08

to bare one's teeth by raising the upper lip

Threat. This gesture, when it is used by a man, shows that he is the equal of his dog.

Edgar Allan Poe alludes to this same gesture in *The Narrative of Arthur Gordon Pym*:

He still obstinately lay in the bottom of the boat; and, upon reiterating the questions as to the motive, made use only of idiotic gesticulations, such as raising with his forefinger the upper lip, and displaying the teeth which lay beneath it. These were black.

11.09

to click one's thumbnail against one's teeth, the nail turned toward the mouth

Refusal. Nothing. Zero.

Dizzy Gillespie in concert in Deauville,
Normandy, France, July 20, 1991.
Photo by Roland Godefroy (full credit on p. 317).

12

THE CHEEKS

*The cheeks are ambivalent: they invite both
the slap and the kiss. That is why nature gave us two cheeks:
for twin kisses or a pair of slaps.*

12.01

to tap a slightly inflated cheek
Erotic invitation, accompanied by a wink.

12.02

to flatten an inflated cheek with a push of the hand
Disbelief. Contempt: "That's just hot air."

12.03

to inflate both cheeks
Signifies the obesity of the person being
discussed. The inflation of the cheeks is
often accompanied by a gesture showing the
immensity of the belly.

12.04

*to slap the cheek with the palm of the hand,
which is pressed firmly against the cheek and then
slid down it*
Oath. "I swear it."
Arab world.

12.05

to give little taps to one's inflated cheek with the tip of the index finger, the air escaping in little mock farts
Mockery. Disbelief.

Maïb-Awls responded by blowing up his right cheek and giving it little pushes with his index finger, which made it go braap-braap.
   Jacques Jouet, *The Republic of Maïb-Awls*

12.06

simultaneously pinching both cheeks between the thumb and index finger, pulling downward
Pity. A gesture simulating the wasting away of the body, cheeks hollow from illness.

12.07

to tap one's cheek with one's index finger
Disbelief. "I don't believe you, you're making that up."

12.08

a kiss on the cheek
See 9.10.
Unknown and refused in Asia (Japan), uncommon in England, doubled up in many other places. The number of kisses on the cheek is curiously codified from region to region, sometimes even from family to family.
This little kiss, known as the *bise* in France, often barely brushes the cheek, which spares women the grating of a poorly shaven face and men a mouthful of foundation. The glasses are removed, out of prudence and politeness, when the other person also wears glasses.

12.09

*to brush with one's right cheek the left cheek of
a forward-facing interlocutor, then the left cheek
against the right cheek, while both hands are
placed on the interlocutor's shoulders*

This is the ceremonial "accolade" given by a
person in a position of authority to the person
receiving the reward or honor. This accolade
can go as far as a hug, such as the one that
occurred between Chancellor Gerhard Schröder
and President Jacques Chirac on June 6, 2004,
at Caen (Calvados), a place neither of them had
been sixty years earlier.

12.10

to pinch one's cheek

a. The valuation of a gourmet: "Excellent."
b. Appreciation of a pretty girl. Italy.
c. Contempt. Albania.

12.11

to pull down on one's cheek with one's index finger
To sulk. "He's pulling a face."

12.12

*to point one's index finger at one's cheek, pushing
against it or not, with or without a screwing motion*

a. Admiration: "Oh, what a beautiful girl!" Italy.
b. Mockery toward a homosexual. "What a sissy."
c. Madness. "You're crazy!" This is a variant of
the finger pointed at the temple. Germany.

12.13

to rub one's cheek against the cheek of another
A type of kiss in certain countries in Central
Europe.

These neighbors embrace in the Chechen fashion, hands
on the hips and cheek to cheek.

> Dominique Le Guilledoux, "In Grosny," *Le Monde*,
> January 12, 1995

12.14

*to trace a gash or scar on one's cheek with the
thumbnail, running from the ear to the mouth*
A gesture indicating that the individual being
discussed is a tough customer, a "scarface."
Southern Italy.

12.15

*to pinch someone's cheek between the thumb and
index finger*
A gesture both affectionate and condescending.
This gesture is often remembered of Napoleon,
who used it on the soldiers of his Old Guard,
whom he treated like grown children.

12.16

to crease one's cheek by pulling the lips to one side
Disbelief; sarcastic and mocking mimicry.

12.17

to slap one's cheek with the palm of one's open hand
Admission of stupidity. Blunder. "Am I ever a fool.
I deserve a slap!"

12.18

to raise an open hand as if threatening a slap
Threat.
The suggestion of this gesture is often followed
by a veritable slap.

Out of severity that joined gesture to reproach, he had more
than once made me familiar with the vigor of his arm and the
loud slap of his large hand.

    Rodolphe Töpffer, *Genevese Tales*

12.19

*one's hand placed next to one's face, the fingertips
joined together and then abruptly opened with a
verbal "pop!"*
"He's crazy."
This is a variant of the finger pointed at the temple.
England.

12.20

*one's closed hand rested against one's cheek as if
to hold up the head*
Depression.
An affected posture of reflection and relaxation.
It can also signify feigned attention.

The hand folded half-way back and at rest beside the cheek
is similar to a position of somnolence; and it is a gesture that
we saw little enough of in traditional eloquence, but rather
the gesture belonging to the auditor and the judge, especially
when he reaches a certain level of indifference.

    Alain, *Propos*, 1923

12.21

to place one's finger on a small tattoo located on the left cheekbone
Warning.
In French, this tattooed mark is called the *point de gouape*, which in French argot roughly means "the mark of the hoodlum." The mark has various significations in the hierarchy of criminal circles.

12.22

to lean one's cheek on one's open hand
Sleepiness. This signifies that a speech or lecture is putting you to sleep; that one has a desire to sleep and would happily go to bed.

12.23

to brush against or rub one's cheek from front to back with the back of one's hand
Boredom. This is the gestural translation of the French expression *La barbe!* ("The beard"), which translates as "I'm bored senseless." The gesture mimics the act of shaving.
In Greece, the same gesture signifies disbelief, a gesture corresponding to a verbal *Mon oeil!* ("My eye!") in French or "My foot!" in English, neither of which is familiar to the Greeks.

One of the *manille* players sympathized with Blaisolle and, passing the back of his hand over the sides of his face, gave him discreetly to understand the immense boredom that Monsieur Tormoigne was in the habit of generating.

    Raymond Queneau, *The Last Days*,
    trans. Barbara Wright, 1990

When his back was turned, Cecile looked at him with contempt and passed the back of her dirty hand across her cheek several times.

    Pierre Mac Orlan, *The Song of the Crew*

For an equivalent from the Arab world, see 35.08.

13

THE CHIN

The chin is the seat of authority: the jut of a raised chin is
indisputable, except when it is held by the goatee.

13.01

to swiftly jut one's chin in the direction of a superior
This is the forward movement of the chin that
replaces the military salute when the hands are
occupied, or when conduct does not permit
a regulation salute. This movement of the chin
brings to mind the butt of the ram, which helps
to explain the name given by the French to this
handless salute: the *coup de bouc*, or "the billy
goat's head-butt."

13.02

to raise one's chin while slightly throwing back
one's head
Refusal. "No."
Greece.

13.03

to boldly jut one's chin toward another
An insolent way of pointing someone out to
one's interlocutor.

13.04

to boldly jut one's chin toward one's interlocutor
Threat.

13.05

to raise one's chin
Superiority, domination. With this movement
of the chin, one looks down on one's interlocutor,
and affirms the superiority and authority one
holds over him or her.

13.06

to turn one's chin in a particular direction
A casual way of indicating where something or
someone might be found, for example when
one's hands are full.

13.07

to lift one's chin and wag it from right to left
Mockery. A way of poking fun at someone without
the use of a finger. In French, this is known
as *faire la nique*, which is borrowed from the
German *nicken*, "to nod the head."

To wag the chin is mockery, contempt we show to someone
by certain gestures that bear witness, and in particular by
lifting and shaking the chin.
  Antoine Furetière, 1690

13.08

*the thumb and index finger frame the chin, pulling
it downward*
Sadness. Disgust: "Yuck!"

13.09

*to pass the hand across one's chin forming a point
or triangle*
a. Forms the shape of a beard on the chin, less
to designate someone with a beard than to
express one's boredom or an unpleasantness.
See also the "beard" comment in 12.23.
b. The same gesture in the Arab world is a sign
of respect, the beard being a sign of wisdom.
See also 35.08.

13.10

*one's hand held flat, palm up, a certain distance
below one's chin, as if to indicate the length
of a beard*
Prolonged boredom. "I grew a beard this long!"

13.11

*with the hand quivering below one's chin as if to
imitate a trembling beard*
a. Senility. An accusation of old age and feeble-
mindedness: "He's such a graybeard."
b. This gesture can also be in imitation of the
billy goat, and of his goatee, often imitated
for purposes of mockery with a vocal bleating:
"Baaaaa."

13.12

*one's thumb and index finger framing the tip
of one's chin*
Beauty. By this gesture one indicates the
fineness of the features of the woman about
whom one is speaking.
Italy, Greece, the Mediterranean world.

13.13

the hand folded back over the palm, fingers stroking the bottom of one's chin from back to front

Mocking denial. To stroke one's chin in this way is similar to wagging the chin (see also 13.07), to rile or nettle someone. Children: "Nanny nanny goat!" or "Nana nana boo-boo!"

13.14

to tap one's chin with the index and middle fingers (or sometimes with the four fingers minus the thumb)

Mockery. Refusal.

"... And you expect me to listen to a comic like you? Nothing doing," she concluded, tapping her chin with the two first fingers of her right hand.

> Raymond Queneau, *The Sunday of Life*,
> trans. Barbara Wright, 1977

13.15

to caress the point of one's chin from side to side with a slightly folded index finger

Refusal. "No, I couldn't care less."
Italy.

13.16

to scratch one's chin just below the lip with the index and middle fingers

Offensive mockery. A gestural equivalent of tapping the chin (see 13.14). Disbelief.

13.17

to pass one's flat hand across one's face, making
it slide from the forehead (thought) to the mouth
(speech), and finally to the chin, which is grasped
with the fingertips
A promise.
Arab world.

13.18

the hand at chin height, fingers together,
the palm cupped
To speak with frankness, proof of being good-
hearted and sincere. In French, to speak *le coeur*
sur la main, "with one's heart on one's hand."

Come now, speak frankly, and show your good-heartedness.
(He raised hand to chin height, his fingers gathered together,
his palm cupped, as if his heart were about to leap into it.)
  Jules Renard, *Pinched Smiles*, 1890

13.19

the index finger pointed beneath one's chin,
accompanied by a smile or pout
Suggestion of homosexuality (for a man),
of effeminacy.

13.20

to stroke below the chin with one's thumb,
hand closed
Provocation: "Good job, nice one." A common
gesture among children.

13.21

to lift the chin of one's interlocutor with one's
index finger
Encouragement. "Don't let them beat you;
keep your chin up!"

13.22

the four fingers together, below the chin, and then flicked forward from back to front
Refusal. Wagging the chin. Disbelief.

13.23

the hand below the chin, applied with some or little pressure, and a light horizontal motion
Exasperation. "I've had it up to here!" Sick and tired. A variant of the gesture with the hand atop the head (1.21 and 1.22).

13.24

the hand open and waving, thumb touched to the chin
This gesture has the same signification as "thumbing the nose," which it resembles.
A gesture of refusal.
South America.

13.25

pensive posturing
A pensive posture is usually affectation. Other than that of Rodin's *The Thinker*, this posture is almost never involuntary or spontaneous. "Thinking" is a spectacle we like to share with those who surround us; it is exceptionally photogenic.

13.26

without laughing, the two partners grasp one another's chin between thumb and index finger
A French children's game that is accompanied by the following song:

> I hold you and you hold me
> By the hairs of our goatees
> The first of us to let out a chuckle
> Gets a little smack right on the knuckle!

14

THE NECK

One of the most fragile parts of the human body.
We are always hesitant to come too close to it:
the hand that reaches out for a caress is tempted to strangle.

14.01

the hand open, laid flat, or the index held out on
its own, as if a blade slitting the throat

a. Threat of death
This threatening gesture can be made in two
parts: 1. Index finger over one's mouth ("Silence.
Keep the secret"). 2. The gesture of slitting one's
throat ("Or else I will cut your throat").
Also known in France as the *sourire Kabyle*,
or "Kabylian smile," which sits somewhat lower
down than the "Glasgow smile."

"These files can be opened only on the Sovereign's orders," said
the archivist. "Anyone breaking the rule has his head cut off."
    He drew the edge of his hand across his throat.
    Ismail Kadare, *The Palace of Dreams*,
    trans. Barbara Bray, 1993

b. More simply, this gesture can indicate that one
is cutting a conversation short: "That's enough.
Shhhh. Zip it!"

14.02

both hands curled into claws and brought to
one's throat
Anger. "I'm going to lose it."

14.03

the hand open below one's throat as if holding a goiter
Disbelief. "Do you take me for a fool? I don't believe you."
South America.

14.04

to bring one's hand to one's throat
This gesture has several meanings:
a. Threat. "I'm going to strangle you!"
Arab world.
b. A warning: "You're going to get arrested, they're liable to put you in chains."
South America.
c. Feigned despair and mockery. "I can't take this, I'm going to hang myself." When a situation doesn't turn out well.
d. Exasperation. "I've had enough!"
Italy.

14.05

one's right hand is brought toward one's throat and grabs the collar of one's garment
Anxiety. A gesture of eloquence that has become common.

14.06

to grasp one's throat while calling for help
This is a call for help when someone is choking on something lodged in his or her throat. This gesture, which can lead to confusion, is still the one recommended by the American Red Cross when in need of help.

14.07

to slide one's hand between the neck and the collar of one's shirt
Signal. Be careful, you're being cheated; don't trust that person.
Italy.

14.08

the index finger slid between one's neck and one's collar as if to open it
Relief. "It was getting pretty hot." Giving oneself some air after a scare.

14.09

to straighten one's necktie with a look of satisfaction
Satisfaction. "I'm the clever one, I got you there."

14.10

to shake one's necktie in the direction of one's interlocutor
Mockery of satisfaction. "You didn't get me!"

14.11

to hold one another by the neck
Friendship. A common gesture of camaraderie.
The Mediterranean world.

14.12

to flick the neck of a friend
Invitation. A very familiar, informal gesture,
bordering on rudeness, which means: "Let's go
get a drink."

14.13

to scratch the nape of one's neck
Seduction. This gesture on the part of a man
signifies that he wants to spend time with the
woman he has met.
Lebanon.

14.14

*to lightly tap the nape of one's neck with
one's hand*
Suggestion of homosexuality (male).
Middle East.

14.15

to place the hand on one's neck, behind the ear
a. Dismay. With this gesture, one is looking to
be comforted.
b. It can also signify that one is holding back
his or her anger.

14.16

*to grasp one's Adam's apple between the thumb
and index finger*
Skinniness.
With this gesture, one signifies that the
designated person has a skinny neck, that he
is a weakling.
Italy.

14.17

the hand held horizontally at the height of the Adam's apple

Satiety. "I'm stuffed right up to here, I couldn't fit another bite."

"It was so delicious that I stuffed myself with it up to here."

He placed one hand on the level of his Adam's apple.

"All the more so," he continued, "seeing that there was this much on the plate."

He placed the other hand in a position thirty centimeters above the table.

"After," he added, "it was all I could do to get a piece of cream cake like this down me."

With both hands he rapidly described a sector of a spherical disc ten centimeters high, with a radius of twenty centimeters and an angle at the center of a hundred and twenty degrees.

Raymond Queneau, *The Sunday of Life*, trans. Barbara Wright, 1977

14.18

to place one's hand on another's neck

A gesture of affection, but also of possession. Only lovers hold each other by the neck.

14.19

to flick the side of another's neck

In Russia, this signifies that the designated individual is in a state of inebriation.

In Poland, one taps the side of the neck twice with the index and middle fingers joined together.

Saint Christopher. Line engraving by M. Schongauer.
Image courtesy of Wellcome Library (full credit on p. 317).

15

THE SHOULDERS

One immediately thinks of Sisyphus and of moving day.
The world is a heavy load to bear ...

15.01

one's hand resting on the shoulder (the scapula)
of one's interlocutor, patting it gently
Gesture of protection, of condescending
sympathy on the part of a superior (or someone
who purports to be) toward an inferior
(or someone who is purported to be). Also
signifies conciliation, reconciliation.
This was the gesture effected by George W. Bush
upon the shoulder of Jacques Chirac at the G8 at
Evian on June 1, 2003.

15.02

to apply a clap on the shoulder (or the thigh)
of one's neighbor
A friendly and familiar gesture, sometimes
considered uncouth.

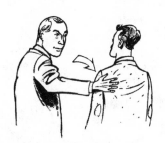

He believed he recognized one of his friends among the
group of *flaneurs* who were always there to watch the
arrival of the stagecoaches, and he approached to give
him a clap on the shoulder, in the manner of the country
gentleman bereft of manners, who, while you are lost in
reveries of your dearest ones, slaps you on the thigh and
asks you, "Do you hunt? ..."

Honoré de Balzac, *Treatise on Walking*, 1833

15.03

to shrug one's shoulders

This gesture has several meanings. It can indicate boredom, disappointment, or contempt. Back in the fourteenth century, the French described it as "shrugging the shoulders as would a Lombard," then, in the sixteenth century, "shrugging the shoulders like an Italian."

In Borneo, a blind beggar counts, with the tips of his fingers, the day's take, shrugging his shoulders in a very Western gesture.

> Jacques Bens, *The Trinity*

His right arm had turned in a quarter circle up next to his head, his hand extended and open most of the way; his mouth stretched out convulsively in the opposite direction, which is to say from right to left, as if to stifle a yawn by hiding it beneath a grimace; and his poor shoulder, which was naturally rather misshapen, spontaneously drew itself closer to his ear, in such a way as to express almost as clearly as would speech an idea that you would translate into casual language as:

WHAT A PITY!

I do not know how familiar you are with physiognomic symptoms; but were you to see a man in such a position, you would be boldly willing to wager that he was bored to death. I would happily match your bet.

> Charles Nodier, *The History of the King of Bohemia and His Seven Castles*, 1830

"One finds Doppelgängers in the pages of German tales, not in real life," says Dupin with a dismissive Gallic shrug.

> Stephen Marlowe, *The Lighthouse at the End of the World*

"Among the Icelandic, a shrug of the shoulders can pass for a smile."

> Jules Verne, *A Journey to the Center of the Earth*

15.04

to raise (shrug) a single shoulder
Boredom.

15.05

to throw one's hand back over one's shoulder
Gesture of rejection.
Nonchalance: "I don't give a damn, it's not at all important."

15.06

to stand side by side, with both parties placing a hand on the outside shoulder of the other from behind the neck
Friendship. Sympathy.

15.07

to slap the shoulder of one's interlocutor while face to face
A gesture of friendship, especially of note among the Inuit.

15.08

to slap one's own shoulder with one's hand
Satisfaction. An amusing method of self-congratulation.

15.09

the hand dusting off one's own shoulder
This gesture, familiar in South America, is one of flattery, and has a similar meaning to the French expression *cirer les pompes* (literally "to wax someone's pumps"), which is not unlike the American "to butter someone up" or, more figuratively, "to kiss someone's rear."

15.10

to throw back one's half-closed hand onto one's shoulder, palm out
Affectation.
A contemptuous gesture signifying that the person in question is pretentious and affected.

15.11

to arch one's shoulders at the same time as holding out one's hands, palms facing up, fingers spread
A gesture accompanied by facial mimicry, eyebrows raised, corners of the lips lowered.
Indifference, helplessness, ignorance.

15.12

to grasp one's shoulders, forearms crossed on the chest (right hand on left shoulder, left hand on right shoulder)
Respectful greeting accompanied by a forward nod of the head.
Asia. Malaysia.

15.13

left arm held out horizontally, right arm folded back on the same plane, the index finger of the closed fist making as if to pull the trigger of a rifle
The shooting of a rifle during the telling of a war story or a tale involving hunting.

I had also to endure the mighty grip of Matifat, great at recounting cynegetical exploits. And what interjections! What onomatopoeia! The call of the partridge, the barking of the dogs, the gun-shots! Then, what gestures! The hand moving like a yawing boat to imitate the zigzags of the game, the back crouching to take better aim, the left arm held out while the right arm goes to the chest to show the gun being brought to the shoulder!

Jules Verne, "Ten Hours Hunting," in *Yesterday and Tomorrow*, trans. I. O. Evans, 1965

15.14

to kiss someone's shoulder

Traditional gesture of respect.

Russia.

"Please have some tea!" he said, gently sighing and respectfully smiling.

And while I was drinking it he quietly came up behind me and kissed me on the shoulder.

Anton Chekhov, *The Shooting Party*,
trans. R. Wilks, 2004

16

THE ARMPITS

And when Nana lifted her arms the golden hairs
of her armpits were observable in the glare of the footlights.
Émile Zola, Nana, trans. anon., 1928

16.01

to tickle under one's arm, or even under both
Mockery, teasing. A reaction to a joke that isn't
funny and for which one must be tickled to
actually laugh.

16.02

to scratch one's head with one hand and one's
armpit with the other
Imitation of a monkey. A gesture of mockery,
often accentuated with verbal mimicry.

16.03

to place one's thumbs under one's arms (at the
armhole of the vest or waistcoat, or under one's
suspenders) while keeping the fingers spread wide
Pride, bravado.

17

THE ARM

*It was something like a great arm thrust
straight out of the ground; at the upper extremity of the arm a
sort of forefinger, supported from beneath by the thumb,
pointed out horizontally; the arm, the thumb, and the forefinger
drew a square against the sky. At the point of juncture of
this peculiar finger and this peculiar thumb there was a line,
from which hung something black and shapeless.*

Victor Hugo, The Man Who Laughs, *trans. anon.*

17.01

*standing straight, feet together, index finger
extended at the end of the arm*
Authority. Command. "Get out of here."

17.02

*to raise one's hand at arm's length and in the
direction of one's interlocutor*
Threat of a blow with the fist or with the
flat of the hand.

17.03

hand at arm's length, palm turned toward one's interlocutor

a. Stop. Halt. This is the gesture the traffic control officer makes to the motorist advancing toward him.

b. This gestural request to stop is not understood everywhere. In the Middle East, it can be interpreted as a friendly greeting. Having been ignorant of this, American GIs killed numerous Iraqis who would not stop because they thought they were being greeted. Other gestures made with the end of the arm are cited in section 22, which is devoted to the hand.

17.04

a cyclist holding his or her arm out horizontally
A warning to other riders: "Beware! Obstacle!"

17.05

to raise both arms
Sign of victory. Satisfaction at having won.

Next came the hardest part: accepting the betrayal, allowing oneself to be flooded with bitterness and disenchantment, giving in to defeat, while the other, arms raised in victory, leaping and jumping, made his way around the ring.

Dominique Muller, *In Spite of Ourselves*

17.06

arms hanging low, with a back-and-forth movement of the hands
Disbelief.
Arab world.

17.07

to jump to one's feet, throwing one's arms in the air
Homage, praise.
A collective gesture (in a stadium, for example).

17.08

to brandish an object at arm's length in a crowd
A collective gesture.
This is the gesture used by the Red Guards,
brandishing Mao's *Little Red Book*.

17.09

both hands raised, making signs to advance or stop,
fingers spread apart at the last moment
Maneuver directions given for civil machinery or
military engines.

17.10

to raise both arms in the air
Surrender. The gesture responding to the order:
"Hands up!"
See also 1.28, "hands placed atop the head."

Arc de Triomphe, August 1944. Image courtesy Special Collections and College Archives, Musselman Library, Gettysburg College.

17.11

both arms extended, forearms bent upward
Greeting.
This was Charles de Gaulle's customary gesture of greeting.
Similar to that of benediction during the parade down the Champs Elysées on August 26, 1944, this gesture found itself accentuated, arms extended, fists closed, for the famous "I understand you" in Algeria in 1958, and caricatured on the poster produced by the Atelier des Beaux-Arts in 1968. This poster took up the pun from De Gaulle's speech in May 1968, in which he said, *La réforme oui, la chie-en-lit non*, which meant both "Reform yes, chaos no," but also "Reform yes, bedshitting no." The Atelier's poster read *La Chienlit C'est Lui*, suggesting he provided both of those things.

... General De Gaulle, in the middle of all those people, makes his way down the Champs Elysées on foot. It looks as if his arms are made of wood.

Emmanuel d'Astier de la Vigerie,
From the Fall of Paris to Its Liberation

17.12

arms open wide, held out toward one's interlocutor
Welcome.
The open-armed welcome leads more or less compulsorily to either the accolade or the embrace.

17.13

both arms spread away from the body, hands flat, palms facing up
Blatancy, obviousness.
Observation that something is obvious or blatant, accompanied by mimicry of surprise.

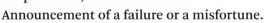

17.14

*to spread both arms from the side of the body
toward the ground*
Helplessness, renunciation.
Announcement of a failure or a misfortune.

17.15

*both hands raised toward the sky, gaze aimed in
the same direction*
Invocation. A gesture of eloquence.

17.16

*arms raised almost completely toward the sky,
hands open, palms up*
Worship. Pleading. A gesture accompanied by
a look toward the sky, head thrown halfway back.
Collective or individual gesture.

17.17

*arms open and allowed to fall, palms facing up,
either standing or kneeling*
Worship. Pleading.

17.18

*to raise both hands in the air, the arms making a
circular shape*
Lift. The signal a foreman gives from the ground
to the machinery operator to order him to lift
the load.

17.19

to wave both hands at the end of outstretched arms
Ignorance. Indifference. "I have no idea; it's all
the same to me."

17.20

*arms raised, hands open, crossing over from left
to right and from right to left*
a. Stop. Finished, over.
b. Refusal, forbidden.

17.21

semicircular movement of the hand and the arm
The signal a foreman gives from the ground
to direct the machinery operator in another
direction.

17.22

both arms spread wide, horizontally
Stop. Finished, over.
Customary signal to stop moving. A gesture
to the machine operator from the foreman on
the ground.

17.23

*the two arms of a priest, facing the altar,
stretched out horizontally*
Offertory.

17.24

*to spread one's arms increasingly wide, starting
at the center of the body, while the gaze is focused
on the interval*
Size. "This wide, and this long ..."

17.25

*arms apart but moving closer together until the
hands touch*
Size. "This narrow, this small ..."

17.26

arms out in front of oneself, forming a circle
Size. Girth. Big belly.

The bus driver, while at a stop, signals to a hesitating fat
woman that she is welcome to board, intimating with
his look and a circular gesture of his arms that if she were
to remain on the platform, the curved guardrail, devoid
of passengers, and against which she could install herself,
would protect her belly from jolts and bumps.

　　Jean Follain, *Paris*

17.27

arms wide, hands fully open
An Italian gesture that suggests "a large rear end."
a. Threat: "Your ass is mine."
b. Luck. In polite conversation, the French
expression *avoir du cul*, which translates literally
as "to have some ass," means "to have good luck."

17.28

to cross one's arms over one's chest
a. Inactivity. Can signify laziness if the gesture
is held long enough.
b. Depending on the situation and the mimicry,
this gesture can also signify defiance, pride.

Monsieur and Madame
Lamélasse,
by Cham, 1839.

17.29

arms held out before oneself, palms open, as if to push something away

a. Horror.

b. This gesture can also signify "Gently. Slow down."

17.30

to raise one's arms to form a V

Victory. Individual or collective gesture.

17.31

arms raised, joining together at the hands on the way up, and shaken together a moment before falling

Triumph. A variant of the previous example. Individual or collective gesture.

17.32

both arms raised

Call for assistance.

From the mountaintop, "Help!"

17.33

both hands raised with arms extended forward, palms facing outward

Compassion, mourning, pain.

Ancient Egypt.

17.34

arms behind the back, both hands touching
Military position of "rest."
A bearing indicating calm and safety.

17.35

both hands in a semicircle in front of oneself,
with a cradling motion
Cradle. Allusion to a baby.

17.36

gesture with both hands imitating the digging
of something with a shovel, followed by a throw
over the shoulder
Disdain. Mockery. "And here's what I think
of that."

17.37

to feign playing an imaginary violin held in the
left hand, the right hand holding the bow
A gesture that makes note of the flatteries
of one's interlocutor.

17.38

to advance, bowing slightly forward, holding
out one's forearm, cutting with one's forward-
facing hand
An authoritative gesture that is made when
"cutting" through the crowd ("Excuse me").
Typically Japanese.

17.39

to run with the arms held out horizontally while imitating the hum of a motor
Imitation of an airplane.
Children's game.

17.40

to run flapping the extended arms up and down
Imitation of a bird.
Children's game.

17.41

arms held aloft, hands open, wiggling the fingers
Imitation of the wind.

The old woman stretched out her arms, opened her hands on high and fluttered her fingers as if imitating the wind.

Antonio Tabucchi, *It's Getting Later All the Time*, trans. Alastair McEwan, 2006

17.42

to raise one's arms, pulling on an invisible toilet chain
Garbage. Something smells bad. See also 7.28.
England.

17.43

to stretch one's arm horizontally out of a vehicle

"Do not pass," when the vehicle is not equipped with visible blinkers (horse carriage, bicycle, etc.).

Announcement that the vehicle is about to turn to the side indicated by the arm.

17.44

to raise one's arm, thrusting it out boldly in front of oneself, with the momentum of the body

Military gesture. An order to attack. "Forward march! Attack!"

This is the gesture of the officer urging the infantrymen forward from the trench to assault the enemy.

This gesture was reproduced on a famous Abel Faivre poster for war bonds issued by the French in support of the war effort in 1916.

On les aura! it said, or "We'll beat them!"

Poster advertising the second national defense loan, 1916, by Jules Abel Faivre.

17.45

to hold an ignited lighter at arm's length

a. Silent demonstration of homage, protest, or mourning.

b. Collective gesture made during rock concerts.

18

THE FOREARM

Radius and Cubitus are in a boat.
Nobody falls into the water.
Explain why.

18.01

the forearm bent so as to make the biceps jut
out visibly
Strength.
This demonstration of force can often lead
to someone squeezing the biceps to feel their
size and hardness.

18.02

to slap one's open right hand against the biceps
of the left arm while holding forward the forearm
with its closed fist
The *bras d'honneur* in France ("arm of honor"),
also known as "the arm," "the Iberian slap,"
or "the Italian salute."
This is the most widely used obscene gesture.
The forearm symbolizes the erect member.
There are numerous variants. For example,
instead of raising the fist, the forearm can be
loosened frontward and horizontally, the hand
flat, palm up; in another version, the forearm
isn't raised all at once, but can be vigorously
shaken on its way up.

This gesture originated in the Mediterranean region. In Malta, it is forbidden. In Hungary, it is known by the name *Lófasz*, which translates literally as "horse dick."

In Jacques Tati's first film, *Jour de fête*, François the mailman makes the gesture of "the arm of honor" every time someone mentions American postmen to him.

One advances the right arm in the direction of the person whom one wants to honor. Then, with a lively and decided gesture, the left hand is slapped on the right biceps. The forearm, rigid, as if moved by a winch, is raised up, the right fist being held energetically closed.

This greeting can often suffice on its own, but sometimes it is accompanied by verbal imprecations that are varied, but generally all follow the pattern "Go (blank) yourself."

Yvan Audouard, *Le Canard Enchaîné*, November 29, 1972

"Tell me," said the old woman, "is it true? Are things going so badly for him that he's come to shut himself away here?"

The young caballero made a gesture as if to say, "we'll talk about that later!" Then, having leapt up the steps to rejoin his companions, who were busied around the truck, he turned back beneath the light of a parking lamp, pressed his left hand against the crook of his arm and raised his heavy fist, saying:

"I'm telling you, Mama, he'll get what he deserves, and all the way in."

Jacques Perret, *A General Passing By*

Mr. George Rubel, twenty-eight years old, copy editor, has been levied a fine of 300 F for having made, with his arm, an unseemly gesture addressed to the police forces assembled on Boulevard Saint-Germain, where he happened to be passing on his moped without having participated in the protest.

Le Monde, June 26, 1973

18.03

to launch the closed fist forward while the left hand strikes the crook of the arm
Obscene gesture, a variant of the previous example. The gesture in this case does not allude to the erection, but rather to penetration.

18.04

to feign to brush one's sleeve with the closed right fist
Flattery, from the French expression *passer la brosse à reluire*, literally "to shine with a soft brush." Similar to "buttering someone up," or perhaps "to rub someone the *right* way."

18.05

the fingers of the left hand holding up the right elbow, the right forearm extended vertically, its fingers pivoting on the wrist
Madness. Mocking gesture.
Southern Italy.

18.06

to throw the open right hand before oneself as if throwing something
Contempt.
A gesture of eloquence used by the orators of antiquity.

18.07

one's forearm and open hand seem to throw something back over one's shoulder
Indifference. "To the Devil with him!"

18.08

elbows against the torso, both forearms extended with hands spread
Helplessness. Renunciation. "Nothing I can do about it."

18.09

the hand (palm down) and the forearm brought together make a back-and-forth gesture in front of the body
Prostitution. "She's a working girl."
South America.

18.10

to swing one's raised forearm from right to left and vice versa
A negative gesture, known in France as the *coup d'essuie-glace*, or "the windshield wiper," indicating that one will no longer continue to bid in an auction.

18.11

one's left forearm folded back over one's chest while the right arm is extended to indicate a direction, both hands facing that same way
Traffic signal. The customary gesture of the traffic control officer used to direct traffic in an intersection.

18.12

one's forearm folded back over one's face
Fear of impending blows.
This gesture can be translated as demonstrating actual or feigned fear.

18.13

quick movement of one's forearm and open hand before one's face
Contempt. Negation: "It's worthless."

To discover a group of livid men, a yellow star sewn to their jackets, confined in a hangar (bound for what destination?), confined, hunted, and about whom, with hearts clenched, we questioned the guard (or the Wächter) who accompanied us, receiving in response a gesture of the hand, quick, moving downward, as if to chase away a fly, at the same time as the wonderful man spat out, "Ach! *Polnisch!*" or "Ach! *Jude!*" ... That said it all.

René de Obaldia, *Exobiography*

18.14

from back to front, one's hand accompanies the movement of a person who is being invited to pass ahead
Politeness. Gesture generally effected by the motorist and directed to the pedestrian:
"Go ahead, please, I insist."

19

THE ELBOW

*It is lifted and made use of just long enough
to produce a little grease.*

19.01
to strike one's elbow against the table
Avarice. "What a cheapskate!"
Uruguay. South America.

19.02
*to tap one's elbow with the palm of the
opposite hand*
a. Same signification as the previous example.
South America.
b. In Germany and Austria, this gesture signifies
that the designated person is an imbecile.

19.03
*the left hand energetically striking the right elbow
while the right hand makes as if to slice through
the air in front of it, moving downward*
To turn away, to drive out.

19.04

to solidly strike one's right elbow with one's left hand, the forearm of the right arm raising a clenched fist
Obscene gesture.
Aggressiveness. Defiance.
Italy.

19.05

the left hand striking the right elbow, the raised forearm of which shakes its hand, palm facing backward
Obscene gesture.
A variant of the previous example, this gesture combines the rejection to the rear with that of the raised elbow.

19.06

one's arm folded horizontally in front of oneself, the palm of the right hand tapping or smacking the elbow of the left arm, which is also folded horizontally in front of oneself
Alert; exert caution. This gesture signifies to one's interlocutor that he or she must beware of possible treachery.
Netherlands.

19.07

with arm bent, to quickly bring the elbow up and then thrust it in the direction of one's interlocutor
Threat. Retaliation. The insulted or threatened individual thus signifies that he or she is prepared to defend him- or herself, at the very least, and to fight.

19.08

*to mimic the movements of bird wings with one's
hands in front of the chest, raising and lowering
them bent at the elbows*
Gesture accompanied by clucking like a chicken.
Cowardice: "You're such a chicken."
North America.

19.09

*a discreet jab of the elbow into the waist of
one's neighbor*
One makes this gesture to attract the
interlocutor's attention, thereby signaling that
he or she has missed something.

Frédéric turned toward Pellerin. The artist responded by an
abundance of gestures, the whole of which signified, "Ah,
my friend, they have rejected me. The Devils! So be it."

Thereupon, Frédéric jabbed Regimbert with his elbow.
"Yes! So true! It is time! I must be going!" And Regimbert
stepped up onto the platform.

Gustave Flaubert, *Sentimental Education*

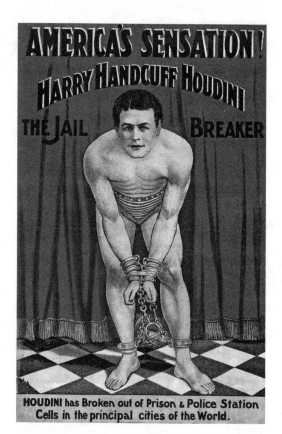

"Harry Handcuff Houdini." Image courtesy of Billy Rose Theatre Division,
The New York Public Library. Available through the New York Public Library Digital Collections
at http://digitalcollections.nypl.org/items/b5cfbf49-a59e-7548-e040-e00a18060aef
(accessed November 14, 2017).

20

THE WRIST

*The wrist, which connects the rigid forearm to the
flexibility of the hand, is an engineering success story for which
the Creator, who by the way made a royal mess of the spinal
column, can for once be proud. Thanks to the wrist, a number
of gestures are possible, and while the skill needed to effectuate
them is indeed "all in the wrist," make sure not to confound
them, or you might end up getting yours slapped.*

20.01
*while standing, the left hand holds the wrist of the
right hand*
Remembrance, reverence.

20.02
*to raise one's right wrist and strike it with the
left hand*
Departure. Flight.
Depending on the speed or liveliness of the
movement, this gesture can signify "He took off,"
or "We're out of here, we're gone," or even,
"Get lost, take off, beat it!"

20.03
to let one's wrist hang and to shake it limply
Suggestion of homosexuality. Effeminate
mannerisms. "Limp-wristed."

20.04

to raise the right hand limply while slapping the right wrist with the left hand

Same signification as the previous example. This accusatory gesture seems to be mostly in use in the Netherlands.

In Turkey, to have an erection.

20.05

to place the edge of the right hand against the wrist and slide the hand up bit by bit until it reaches shoulder height

Criticism of the insatiability of another.

"Give him an inch, he'll take a mile." In French, *en vouloir long comme le bras*, which literally means "wanting it as long as your arm."

20.06

to fully raise the arm of a winner, grasping it by the wrist

Public homage or tribute.

20.07

to mimic masturbation with the right hand

Obscene and insulting gesture.

Sometimes the person effecting this gesture will spit in the palm of the hand before closing the fist. This gesture is known as the *Veuve Poignet* in France, which translates literally as "the widow's wrist."

20.08
the left hand grasps the wrist of the right hand,
the right fist closed, and shakes it
Obscene and insulting gesture.
A variant of the *bras d'honneur* (see 18.02).
Mediterranean world.

20.09
the right wrist, fist clenched, slides back and forth
in the open left hand, which is wrapped around it
Obscene gesture. Masturbation.
A variant of the *bras d'honneur* (see 18.02).
Middle East.

20.10
one hand grasps the wrist of the other and slides
up and down along it
Obscene gesture.
Sex. Masturbation.

20.11
to cross one wrist over the other as if they were
bound together
Surrender. "I yield, I'm your prisoner."

20.12

to mimic turning a key in a lock
To close. To lock. To imprison.

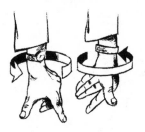

20.13

to rotate the wrist, hand half-open
To steal. Suggests a thief.
A gesture imitating a pickpocket.

20.14

to feign slitting the artery of the left wrist with the
thumbnail of the right hand
Suicide.

"Well, as soon as there is the faintest hint of wrinkles
underneath these eyes ... as soon as this lofty figure starts
to fall apart ... Sliiiiiice!" ... she made the gesture of
opening a razor and slitting the artery of her left wrist.
    Lucien Boyer, *How It Was Beautiful, My Town*

20.15

to cross one's wrists, palms out front, fingers lightly
bent, pinky fingers joined in a hook, then to quickly
separate the two hands
Suspicion. Distrust toward another.
Southern Italy.

20.16

at the end of an extended or slightly bent arm, the wrist makes the hand turn in one direction, then the other
Indecision; hesitation. "More or less. Six of one, half a dozen of the other."

20.17

the hand resting on the wrist, to tap on a table with one, two, or three fingers
Impatience. Irritation.

20.18

to pivot the two hands on the wrists with the forearms held aloft vertically
A children's game in France, which is accompanied by a little song:

> That's what they do, do, do
> The little marionettes,
> That's what they do, do, do
> Three little turns and they're through.

20.19

to tap on a watch worn on the left wrist with the index finger of the right hand
Tardiness. "Hurry up, we're running late!"

21

THE FINGERNAILS

It's best to know your gestures well—
from the top of your head right down to your toenails.

21.01

to hold out both hands, palms facing down,
in such a way that all ten fingernails are visible
Proof of cleanliness.
Especially in boarding schools, students are
asked to present their fingernails, the cleanliness
of which is verified by a schoolmaster.

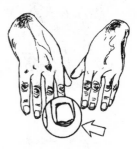

The last students of the class, standing in a line, were
invited to present the fingers of both hands, and smack!
Right on the fingernails! What made the cane special
was that it would not break, but instead divide into very
thin sprigs, the bundle of which, when wielded by an
expert, produced a highly effective lashing.
    André Billy, *The Luxembourg Terrace*

To present ten neat fingernails instead of five, now that's a
beautiful thing.
    Isidore Ducasse, May 22, 1869

21.02

to make a cracking noise with one's fingernail
against the edge of one's teeth
Refusal. Nothing.
This gesture can signify that its maker possesses
nothing, or that his or her interlocutor will
obtain nothing.
Europe and the Arab world.

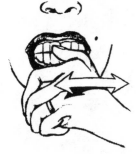

21.03

to rub the thumbnail on one's teeth, the length of the jaw
Refusal. Nothing.
Variant of the previous gesture.

21.04

to make a popping noise by placing one's thumbnail below the teeth of one's upper jaw and snapping it with a quick movement
Threat. Anger. Provocation.
Mediterranean insult.

21.05

to kiss one's thumbnail, which is then quickly moved away from the lips
Oath. "I swear it to you."
This kiss takes the place of one that would be placed on a crucifix.
Spain. South America.

21.06

to nervously chew one's fingernails
Nervousness.
Alongside the appropriate mimicry, this gesture signifies that one's interlocutor or another person is making one nervous with his or her behavior or speech.

21.07

to nibble one's thumbnail
Irritation. Impatience.

21.08

to strike one thumbnail against the other with both
fists clenched
Ridiculous mock applause made in derision.

21.09

to press one thumb against the other and turn
lightly, as if to crush an insect
Mockery. Superiority. "I would crush you like
a bug."
Spain.

21.10

to blow on the fingernails of one hand and then rub
them against the lapel of one's jacket
Self-satisfaction, brought about by being correct
or having succeeded.

22

THE HAND

The hand is the instrument of instruments.
Aristotle, De Anima

The part of the human body at the end of the arms, which nature has given to man in order to make him capable of the many sorts of Arts and Fabrications.

Furetière, *Universal Dictionary*, 1690

[Among men], the terminal organ of the upper limb, formed by an enlarged and articulated area attached to the forearm and terminating in five appendages (the fingers), each of them articulated at several points and one of which (the thumb) is opposable to the four others; organ that forms the principal natural instrument of touch and prehension and, by this fact, a particular means to knowledge and action. Synon. *Paw, palm, fist, mitt.*

INALF—Institut National de la Langue Française

The five fingers of the hand.
Illustration by Jean Veber.

And what of the hands? We require, we promise, call, dismiss, threaten, pray, supplicate, deny, refuse, interrogate, admire, number, confess, repent, fear, shame, doubt, instruct, command, incite, encourage, swear, testify, accuse, condemn, absolve, abuse, despise, defy, vex, flatter, applaud, bless, humiliate, mock, reconcile, recommend, exalt, entertain, delight, complain, sadden, comfort, despair, astonish, exclaim, quieten; what can we not do with them? A variation and multiplicity that is the envy of the tongue.

    Montaigne, *Essays*, II, 12

The hand, which we use to eat, to drink, to wash ourselves, to do our hair, to open and close the door, to piss, to make the sign of the Cross and the military salute.

    Pierre Bettencourt, *The Littrérama, or The Triumph of the Free Wheel*

I recognize my right hand by its position: it is to my right; and my left hand is to my left. There are exceptions, such as this one: at this moment, your right hand is to my left, and my right is your left. In Roman antiquity, men held their togas with their right hand, and women their clothing in their left: we didn't even invent the position of the buttons on our clothing.

And to this day, in certain countries that are more theocratic than democratic, the thief's hand is cut off. This mutilation makes it completely pointless to consult this particular dictionary entry. All gestures are done with the right hand, the left being reserved for impure tasks; left-handed people should not expect other counsel from me.

We know many types of hands, and notable among them:

- *The hand of justice.* This was one of the symbols of royalty, placed at the extremity of the royal scepter. The hand of justice was a small hand of ivory, open, with raised fingers; it symbolized judicial power, the primary power of the royalty. The coins of Louis X, who was appropriately known as The Headstrong, were the first to feature the scepter with its hand of justice.
- *The votive hand.* A hand of bronze or marble that, in Greco-Roman antiquity, was offered to a god in hopes of obtaining a pardon or to give thanks for an honor.
- *The hand of glory.* This is the dried hand of a man who has been hanged, a candle placed between its fingers, to which we

used to attribute magical powers, notably the power to immobilize those who were touched by the light of the candle's flame.

- *The hand of Fatima.* The daughter of Muhammad, Fatima was born in 606 CE. Her hand is a talisman of protection against the evil eye; it symbolizes Providence, and integrates the five fundamental precepts of the law of the Prophet, which correspond to its five fingers. The hand of Fatima is largely carried by women, for instance in the form of a pendant.

- In French, a quire of paper (or twenty-five sheets) is known as *une main de papier*, or "a hand of paper." Twenty quires make up a ream, just as twenty *mains* make up *une rame*.

- *Buddha's hand.* This citron fruit, grown in warm climes, is a variety whose fruit is segmented into finger-like appendages that take a shape similar to that of the human hand. In many Asian countries, it is known as the Buddha's hand. The fragrant fruit is used for perfuming rooms in China, and is also given as an offering in Buddhist temples. For these offerings, Buddhists tend to prefer fruits where the fingers are closed, thus mimicking closed hands in the act of prayer. This hand is a symbol of contentment, longevity, and luck.

The use of the hand goes back to the earliest days; for a Christian example, Adam was warned not to "put forth his hand, and take also of the tree of life, and eat." Not too long after, Adam's son made use of his hands, too: "And now thou art cursed from the earth, which hath opened her

John II the Good of France.

Hand of Fatima pendant, Morocco, ca. 1850. Image courtesy of the Minneapolis Institute of Art, the Christina N. and Swan J. Turnblad Memorial Fund, Accession Number 91.141.17.

mouth to receive thy brother's blood from thy hand." We must be wary of our hands. We often *give someone a hand*, but often enough someone *bites the hand that feeds him*. And don't forget, *the devil finds work for idle hands*.

The constituent parts of the hand, other than the fingers, are the ulnar side, the palm, the flat of the hand (the palm and fingers not folded), and the back of the hand.

And the three musketeers join
The five fingers of the hand
Steer the tiny submarine
In search of their homeland

    Jacques Prévert

Hermann-Paul,
"Jeux de mains," *Le Sourire*, 1900.

22.01

to wave one's hand at the end of one's extended arm, higher to lower, palm facing front
Hello. Goodbye.

This may be the last day of my life.
I raised my right hand in salute to the Sun,
But I didn't salute it as if to say goodbye—
No, instead to signal I was happy to see that
this was all.

    Fernando Pessoa, *Poems of Alberto Caeiro*

22.02

*hand raised at the end of a partially or fully
extended arm*
Approval of a question asked. To vote with a
raised hand.

For reasons that are in no way political, I prefer an open
hand to a closed fist; this symbol appealed greatly to Nehru,
in whom I found a very friendly supporter.
    Le Corbusier

In Chandigarh (Punjab), Le Corbusier erected
an open hand that stood fifty feet high.

Le Corbusier's *La Main
ouverte* monument
in Chandigarh, India.

22.03

*to spread the five fingers of one's hand in mimicry
of rays of light*
Awe. Radiance.

"*L'era un masnà, con due oci, pff!*" He was a rascal with that
certain sort of eyes ... and he spread five fingers to show
the radiance lost over time, two blue and lively eyes in the
indistinct magma of memory.
    Rosetta Loy, *The Bicycle*, 1974

22.04

*hand raised, fingers apart,
directed toward one's adversary*
Curse.
Mediterranean world.

22.05

hand raised, palm to the front,
fingers slightly spread
Friendly greeting addressed to someone a ways
off, or someone caught in a crowd.

22.06

hand held out, palm to the front
Gesture used by antiracist movements.
In France, as a yellow symbol, this can be
translated as "Don't touch my friend."
Gesture initiated by SOS Racisme in
November 1984.

22.07

palm of the hand whitened (with paint),
held forward at arm's length
Peace.
This gesture is made in crowds during large
pacifist demonstrations that denounce any
violent behavior.

22.08

hand held flat at the end of one's arm,
palm faced earthward
Roman greeting showing that there is no weapon
in one's hand.
Adopted by fascist movements in Italy, Spain,
and Germany, with some variation.

22.09

hand held aloft, palm of the hand facing front
Fascist salute.
In Germany, it was accompanied by
the interjection *"Heil!"*; in Italy, by the
interjection *"Eya!"*

22.10

*arm bent, forearm held vertically, palm of the hand
facing forward*
Fascist salute used by Adolf Hitler. A brief
gesture, a variant of the Roman salute that was
particular to the Führer.

22.11

arm held out to the front, palm facing down
Salute of a political leader to the crowd
acclaiming or cheering for him or her.

22.12

*to raise the forearm, palm of the hand turned
toward the crowd*
Benediction, blessing.

22.13

*small wave of the hand made by the Queen of
England*
A unique gesture, personal, inimitable.

Queen Elizabeth II in
Brisbane, Australia, 1954. State
Library of Queensland image.

White House photo
by Eric Draper.

22.14

to turn halfway back while moving away, making a small gesture with the open right hand, which is waved in the direction of those who have been left
Small gesture frequently made by George W. Bush.

22.15

hand open, held toward the lens of a camera
Unequivocal refusal.

22.16

military salute
See in 2.07 the memorandum written by General Poillöüe de Saint-Mars.
There are as many different salutes as there are national armies. The right hand touches the kepi, the cap, or other headwear, sometimes horizontally, sometimes held flat, the five fingers squeezed together and facing the superior to whom the salute is being made.

Along the roads, the Kirdi slap their thighs with the palm of the right hand and then give a military salute. Their version of the African soldier's salute. The militiamen's wives also do this ... (January 28 [1932]).
> Michel Leiris, *Phantom Africa*, trans. Brent Hayes Edwards, 2017

22.17

hand held out to the front, palm open, and slowly turned in the shape of a cup or bowl
To offer something.

22.18

to gently shake the fingers of one's hand in front of oneself, or slightly off to the side
Danger avoided, both literally and figuratively. "That was a close one! What a close shave!"

22.19

the hand held out, flat, oscillating before oneself
Hesitation, indifference. "Maybe. I won't say yes, but I'm not saying no."

22.20

hand flat, its edge facing the chest, oscillating from right to left
Hesitation.
"I'm on the fence. Six of one, half a dozen of the other."

22.21

hand open at shoulder height, palm facing front, slightly waving
Gesture of denial or refusal.

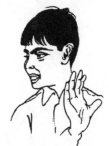

22.22

hand held flat at arm's length, the four fingers folded and unfolded several times
Greeting. Hello and goodbye, from a distance. In one variation, the four fingers are waved successively.

22.23

one's hand raised and directed toward one's interlocutor, fingers folded onto the palm several times
Invitation: "Approach, come closer."
Japan.

22.24

the same gesture, but effectuated with the arm pointed toward the ground
The same invitation as above, but more discreet.
Japan.

22.25

to flutter one's dangling hand up and down
Dismissal. "Go away!"

22.26

palm of the hand flat and even with the shoulder, head thrown back
Oath taking.
Middle East.

22.27

arm bent, forearm raised, palm facing forward, fingers together, hand at shoulder height
Oath taking.

22.28

to raise the forearm, palm facing forward
Oath. This gesture is the swearing in when
testifying before the court: "I swear to tell the
truth, the whole truth, and nothing but the truth."

"With a voice that trembled, but was still beautifully
resonant, Lady Beltham, raising her right hand, said,
"I swear it!"

   Pierre Souvestre and Marcel Allain, *Fantomas*, 1911

22.29

*the left hand placed flat atop a sacred book
(Bible, Quran ...) while the right hand is raised*
A variant of the previous example. Sacred oath.
This is the customary oath in the United States.

22.30

hand raised, palm directed forward
Exhortation. To call for the attention of
those present.
Gesture of eloquence.

22.31

*to present to one's interlocutor the palm of the left
hand, facing up*
The presentation of one's hand to the palm
reader (chiromancer), who will then read the
lines of the hand.

22.32

to place one's flat hand atop a funeral casket
Homage to the deceased. Final farewell.
Variant: In March 2005, a national funeral service
was held for Nicola Calipari, an officer of the
Italian secret service killed in Iraq by an American
patrol while protecting Giuliana Sgrena, a hostage.
The president of the Italian Republic pressed
both his hands flat against the coffin, recently
arrived at the Rome airport, and held them there
at length.

22.33

*to wave an open hand, moving from up to down
and back, fingers close together, palm facing down*
Goodbye.
The gesture of an adult. (See the following for
the corresponding child's gesture.)

22.34

*to wave an open hand at arm's length, palm facing
forward, while opening and closing the fingers and
slowly rotating the wrist*
Goodbye.
The gesture of a child.

22.35

*palm up, the hand flapping its fingers,
which open and close*
a. Call: "Come here!" France, England,
Netherlands.
b. In Italy, a gesture of farewell.

22.36

palm facing down, flapping the four fingers,
which open and close
Call.
Italy, Spain, Tunisia.
The gestures in 22.35 and 22.36 are an example
of the "false friends" that can create confusion.

22.37

hand flat, palm up, held out to one's interlocutor
Challenge: "Would you like to bet?"

22.38

to thrust one's hand forward toward an
interlocutor, palm in front, abruptly spreading
the fingers, as if to make contact with the
other's face
A common insult in Greece, called "the gesture
of *mountza*," made most notably by motorists.
A false friend that the tourist may confuse with
a gesture asking him or her to stop or back up.
The origins of this gesture can be traced
back to the era when criminals were paraded
in the streets; the crowd would throw refuse
in their faces. A sexual connotation would later
be added: the five extended fingers are the
five rapes promised to the sister of the insulted.

22.39

to thrust both open hands into the face of
an adversary, palms facing forward
A variant of the previous example,
only worse, because of the use of two
hands instead of only one.

22.40

to squeeze all one's fingers together while closing the hand
Mockery. This gesture is what seventeenth-century French linguist Antoine Oudin called *faire le cul de poule*, which literally means "to make the chicken's ass."

22.41

a back-and-forth horizontal motion made by the hand in front of oneself
Fornication.

"In how many kingdoms of the world"—(Here Trim kept waving his right hand from the sermon to the extent of his arm, returning it backwards and forwards to the conclusion of the paragraph).

> Laurence Sterne, *The Life and Opinions of Tristram Shandy, Gentleman*, vol. 2, 1759

22.42

to pass one's open hand back and forth in front of one's face as if to cover and uncover it
Negation.
It is the hand in this case that makes the gesture of negation instead of the head, which remains immobile.
Japan.

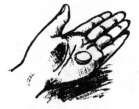

22.43

hand halfway extended horizontally, palm cupped and facing up
Begging.

22.44

hand halfway extended, the palm held flat and the
thumb extended to the side
Demand of payment.

22.45

to hold out one's open hand, palm up, and bend the
fingers up several times
Payment.
South America.

22.46

to hold out one's hand as if to give something
This is sometimes a false gesture; the person
effecting it only feigns to give.

My generosity is a fleeting gesture.
    Colette, *The Break of Day*

22.47

hand held out horizontally, elbow bent at the hip
Refereeing. Tennis: the ball has touched the line,
but it is in.

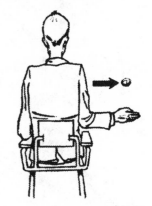

22.48

hand held out, palm forward, as if to push
something away from oneself, while turning the
head in the opposite direction as if not to see
Gesture of eloquence. Aversion. Disgust.
This is the gesture made by Monsieur Bafouillet,
lawyer, in defense of Camember the Sapper.

Le Sapeur Camember.

22.49

hand open, with index, middle, and ring fingers joined together, the thumb and pinky folded back on the palm
Worship. Benediction.
A religious gesture known since antiquity.

22.50

to strike with one's hand the palm of another player, which he or she holds behind him- or herself
Children's game known as "hot hands," "slapsies," "red hands," or simply "slaps."

22.51

to abruptly flip one's hand over at waist height, as if to throw something to the ground
Insult. "That's garbage. It has no importance. I couldn't care less."

22.52

to strike the strings of a racket with the palm of the free hand
In tennis, congratulations addressed to one's adversary.

22.53

to tap one's fingertips on the table
Impatience.

22.54

the hand mimics writing on the corner of a
table in a restaurant
Call. To request the check from the waiter
or waitress.

22.55

the right hand makes a pen with the index finger
and, with this, makes the gesture of writing on the
palm (paper) of the left hand
a. To write. "Write me!"
b. The same gesture can signify "to read,"
the index finger in this case tracing the lines
of an imaginary text on the palm of the
opposite hand.

22.56

the palm of the hand in the shape of a cup or small
bowl, or the fist half-closed in the shape of a cup,
brought to the mouth, the head lightly tipped back
Thirst. Drink.

22.57

the hand laid flat and slid in a semicircular
movement above the plane of the table
Theft.
One makes as if to grab all the money to be
found on the table. But this gesture can also
mean "It is time to pay." South America.

22.58

the hand laid flat and slid in a semicircular movement above the plane of the table
An identical gesture to the previous example, but instead of grabbing up, one mimics displacing a liquid on the table.
To flounder or paddle. To be unable to extricate oneself from a situation. "You're treading water."

22.59

to take an object (a banknote, for example) to one's forehead after having brought it to one's lips
Respectful satisfaction.
Arab world.

To celebrate the beginning of a new year, I give the taxi driver twice the fare of the trip. He looks at the bill, takes it ceremoniously in both slightly cupped hands, gives it a long kiss, then takes it to his forehead, and drives away at full speed out of fear that I might change my mind.
    Paul Fournel, *Cairot Top*

22.60

the right hand, palm flat and turned toward the table, sweeps a large circular area
Gesture of demonstrative eloquence, encompassing everything at once. This gesture was often used by Jacques Chirac.

22.61

the right hand open, its edge brought toward the face of one's interlocutor
Threat of a slap.
The gesture of an adult warning a child.

22.62

the closed hand turning an imaginary crank
handle near the head
Cinema, both literally and figuratively.
This gesture evokes the motion that was
originally used to operate a movie camera
or projector. This is the origin of the expression
"we're rolling," and of the French expression
on tourne (literally "we're turning").

22.63

the hand makes a gesture as if grabbing something
from thin air
Theft: "Beware of thieves."
Italy.

22.64

to open and close one's hand like a beak onto the
thumb, the four other fingers clenched together
above it (the upper part of the beak)
Silence: "Zip it! Be quiet!"

22.65

the hand's fingers are clenched together in a bundle
pointing upward, slightly shaken
Questioning: *"Ma … que … Che vuoi?"* ("What do
you want?")
National gesture of Italy.

22.66

the raised hand falls toward one's interlocutor
Refusal. Negation.
"That's enough out of you! ..."

22.67

*the hand, its fingers clenched in a bundle,
is brought downward*
Failure. Blunder.
Sarcasm: "Almost! A near miss!"

22.68

to lower one's hand toward the ground, palm flat
Size. Small.
This gesture designates the supposed size of the
interlocutor's children.

22.69

*hand raised, the five fingers in an upward-pointing
bundle, the extremities of which are clenched
and unclenched*
Fear. "What a scare! I nearly needed a change
of clothes!"

22.70

*to blow on the ends of one's five fingers,
having clenched them together in a bundle*
Heat. Burn.

22.71

*to raise the right hand and bring it down again
rather quickly, turning the head away as if to
mimic disgust*
Disgust. Disappointment.
"Ach! Scheisse!" Germany.

22.72

*the cupped hand hefts and shakes an
imaginary weight*
Obscene gesture. Insult.
Feigning to weigh the testicles of one's adversary.
In Spanish, this gesture has a name:
huevon ("testicle").
Hispanic world. South America.

22.73

*to touch the nearest wooden object with the
knuckles of one's closed fist or with one's fingertips*
Superstition. To "knock on wood," or *toucher du
bois* in French ("touch wood"). This gesture is
supposed to protect against bad luck.
In some variants, for example in the Netherlands,
one touches underneath a table, where it has
been neither painted nor varnished.

22.74

*the driver of an automobile slightly raises his or
her right hand, the palm remaining in contact
with the steering wheel*
A gesture of politeness to another driver,
frequent in Ireland.
It is often enough to raise the index finger, the
hand remaining on the steering wheel (Europe,
acknowledgment between a heavy truck and a bus).

22.75

to shake one's hand in front of oneself, palm in the air but facing away from one's interlocutor
Greeting. Hello and goodbye.
Typically Italian gesture.

22.76

light rotation of a raised open hand, sometimes preceded by a snap of the fingers
Offhandedness: "I don't care."

22.77

the fingers of the raised hand seem to press against something soft
Cowardice. "Have you gone soft? Are you chickening out?" Gypsy world.

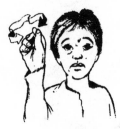

22.78

to raise a partially open hand to face height, the thumb touching the index finger
Reasoning. Argumentation. Demonstration.

22.79

the fingers of the right hand gathered together and touching at their extremities
Reasoning. Argumentation.

22.80
the hand turned back, fingers spread apart in the air, slightly shaken
Gesture accompanied by mimicry of disappointment.
Disappointment. Ignorance: "I have no idea."

22.81
to quickly shake one's hand at face height, its back facing up
Exaggerated surprise.
"You don't say ... Oh boy!"

22.82
one's hand shaped like a grappling hook, the fingers hooked and spread, held forward
To grab; to take to one's advantage.
In the Arab world, this is a gesture of contempt that alludes to scratching the face of one's interlocutor.

22.83
one's closed hand, directed toward one's interlocutor, is suddenly opened, the five fingers spread apart
Dismissal: "Go away! Get lost!"

22.84
with a closed hand, to successively raise the thumb, the index finger, the middle finger, the ring finger, and finally the pinky
To count from one to five.
The fully opened hand adds up to the number five.

22.85

the hand raised (or both hands raised), abruptly opened and closed, directed at a distant interlocutor to whom one wants to communicate certain digits

To count.

The expert and fingersome swain was arrested on the sidewalk, just when he was transmitting some of his signals with six or seven fingers (the hours of love) towards that window on the fifth floor (this, in the opinion of headquarters, was a "strategic feint").

> Carlo Emilio Gadda, *That Awful Mess on the Via Merulana*, trans. William Weaver, 1965

22.86

to fold the thumb to the middle of the palm, then fold the index finger over the thumb to the middle of the palm, then the middle finger, then the ring finger, and finally the pinky

To count.

The Japanese manner of counting from one to five. The series is continued from six to ten with the same hand by successively deploying the fingers in the inverse order, first the pinky finger, then the ring finger, middle finger, index finger and finally the thumb.

22.87

to present one's hand with fingers spread except for the thumb, which is folded back on the palm

Insult. Japan.

These four fingers accuse one's interlocutor of being a pariah, a member of a scorned caste, such as those responsible for the slaughterhouses and butchery.

22.87b
to successively fold down the fingers of the left
hand with the right hand in order to enumerate the
points of an argument from one to five
Argumentation. Counting from one to five.

22.87c
to rap against the table with the back of one's hand
Superstitious gesture in support of a wish:
"Let's hope it works!"
Turkey.

22.5

THE FIST

The union of the five fingers of the hand closed on themselves, the fist is the natural weapon of humankind. It is power, energy, virility, and violence. The gestures of the fist tend to be used more by men; women have historically tended to use them less.

22.88

to brandish the fist, shaking it in the direction of one's interlocutor
Threat.
This is a natural human gesture, understood everywhere. It is accompanied by a furrowing of the brow and verbal threats: "I'll show you, you mouthy numbskull!"

22.89

both fists clenched, forearms bent up
Boxer's stance.
Gesture of threat and aggression.
However, the announced attack can be limited to insults, without going any further.

22.90

to wave a raised fist
Eloquence. Gesture of oration meant to underline the force of one's argument or conviction.

22.91

to hold one's clenched fist before oneself
Avarice, stinginess. Japan.

22.92

to mimic masturbation with a half-closed fist
Obscene gesture.
This is the epitome of the insult in Greece, where one is more typically suggested to be a "jerk-off" than an "asshole."

22.93

fist brandished toward one's interlocutor and shaken back and forth
Obscene gesture. Insult.

22.94

to clench the fist several times with a back-and-forth motion
Obscene gesture.
Insulting refusal.
South America.

22.95

to strike one's left fist with one's right palm,
causing a smacking noise
Obscene gesture that signifies: "I got him, and
right where it hurts."

22.96

to strike one's left fist with the index finger
of the right hand
A variant of the previous gesture. A more
discreet gesture.
Algeria.

22.97

to clench the fists, thumbs up, and mimic the
wringing of a wet rag
Anger; threat to strangle one's interlocutor.

22.98

to hit oneself in the forehead with one's fist
Stubbornness, obstinacy. This signifies that
one's interlocutor is thick skulled, that he does
not understand or refuses to understand.

22.99

to chew on one's closed fist
Anxiety, genuine or feigned.

22.100

to raise the fist of the victor in a violent skyward movement
Victory. True defiance in the face of the vanquished, bordering on an obscene gesture.

Poster from June 1968 in France.

22.101

right (or left) fist raised
Collective international gesture for the rallying of workers movements, and more particularly for communist parties.

In the thirties, before Hitler's rise to power, the dockworkers of Hamburg would salute by raising a fist, accompanied by the words "*Rote Front*" ("Red Front"). For this gesture of salute, they held aloft an open hand, fingers spread, then brought together their fingers, closing the hand. The initial movement symbolized division, the second union.

> Excerpted from a letter written by M. Ajoujes, in *Le Monde*, March 2, 1976

The dictatorship of the proletariat was nothing but empty words, but I think with some sadness of that Spanish Republican officer, in Malraux's *Man's Hope*, who was shot because instead of using the military salute, he raised his fist, unable to tell a lie.

> Robert Escarpit, *Le Monde*, February 14, 1976

22.102

the fist raised fairly high, moving vertically up and down
Speed. "Faster! Hurry up!"

22.103

thumbs inside the fists
Superstition.
One wishes someone "good luck" by quickly
lowering the thumbs. This is equivalent to
crossing the fingers to ward off bad luck.
Germany.

22.104

one's chin rested on one's fist
Contemplative attitude. Pose.

22.105

with elbow bent, to hold out one's forearm,
fist closed, upon which the lady places her wrist
to allow herself to be led
"To offer one's fist to a lady" is an ancient
custom related to chivalry. The woman places
her hand on the closed fist of the knight to
avoid the intimacy of contact.
This can bring to mind the French expression
L'Amour passe le gant (literally "Love passes
the glove"), which Antoine Furetière defined
as: "When one touches the hand of another
unexpectedly, without having had the
opportunity to present it ungloved" (*Universal
Dictionary*, 1690).

After dinner, there I was again, my hand on the fist of
Monsieur de Marseille, off to take in the citadel and the view.
     Madame de Sévigné

Sigognac, bowing slightly, hurriedly presented his fist to
Isabelle, who pressed against the ruffled sleeve of the Baron
the tips of her slender fingers, in such a way as to give to
that delicate pressure an insinuation of encouragement.
     Théophile Gautier, *Captain Fracasse*

22.106

to raise one's fist at arm's length in two movements: elbow against the body, then suddenly thrust toward the sky
Protest; opposition.
This gesture accompanies and supports a slogan chanted by the crowd, particularly in Asia (Korea, Japan).

22.107

fist closed, turned toward the front
Deafness.
Sign Language. (A useful sign to know for those who are not hard of hearing.)

22.108

the clenched fist clutching a stylized rose
Symbol of the socialist parties.

22.109

to smack one's fist into one's palm
a. To vanquish. To smash one's adversary.
b. This is also a sign of impatience.

22.110

*to punch with one fist into the open palm of
one's other hand*
Anger. To control the desire to hit someone
or something.

22.111

—*right fist closed, begin by touching the knuckle
of the index finger* (January: 31 days),
—*then the hollow between the knuckle of the index
finger and that of the middle finger* (February:
28 or 29 days),
—*then the knuckle of the middle finger* (March: 31 days),
—*the following hollow* (April: 30 days),
—*the knuckle of the ring finger* (May: 31 days),
—*the following hollow* (June: 30 days),
—*the knuckle of the pinky finger* (July: 31 days),
—*restart with the index finger* (August: 31 days),
—*as far as the knuckle of the pinky finger*
(December: 31 days).
Mnemonic device used to remember the number
of days in each month of the year.

22.112

*to bump the fist of one's interlocutor with one's
own fist*
Friendly encounter; a gesture equivalent to
the handshake.
Haiti.

Auguste Rodin, *La Cathédrale*, 1908.
Photo by Jean-Pierre Dalbéra
(full credit on p. 317).

23

BOTH HANDS

23.01

both hands forming a large circle
Rude threat.
One's adversary is threatened with "having his ass stretched this wide." See 17.27.
Italy.

23.02

both hands open, arms outstretched
Ignorance: "I have no idea."
A typically Italian gesture, often accompanied by mimicked naïveté.

Bella had watched him, a smile on her lips, with an almost insolent look, her hands open wide.
   Luigi Pirandello, *Our Memories*

23.03

to raise one's empty hands
Innocence; ignorance.
This is also the gesture of the magician.
"Nothing in my hands, nothing in my pockets."

23.04

both hands placed flat on the roof of a car
The position of the offender as he or she is searched by police on the side of the road.
North America.

23.05

to rapidly rub both palms together
Satisfaction; self-contentment.

23.06

to stick up the thumb of one hand while the other hand, flat, is held next to it horizontally
The advertising gesture of the vermouth brand Punt e Mes ("One and a Half") from Turin, at the end of the nineteenth century. The customer made this gesture to order his vermouth in the cafe bars.
Italy.

23.07

both hands connected by the pinky fingers
Imitative gesture: the crab or the spider.

23.08

to cradle both hands before oneself, one placed atop the other, the back of one in the other's palm
Lack of understanding. Hesitation: "I don't understand."
North Africa.

23.09

to turn one hand around the other in front of oneself
a. French children's game: *Tourne tourne petit moulin* ("Turn turn little windmill").
b. Difficulty. Complication. The undertaken action spins in a circle without ever fully getting underway.
South America.

23.10

both hands laid flat on the chest, brought together until the fingers are touching
This gesture is executed with the eyes closed.
Voyage.
This gesture is used in hopes of predicting the future—good if the fingers touch (the voyage will occur); bad if they do not touch (the voyage will not occur).
Bedouin tribes. Arab world.

23.11

the fingers of both hands interlaced, both wrists moving back and forth
Anxiety.
Seeking forgiveness.

23.12

to strike the knuckles of one closed fist with those of the other closed fist
Wager: "I dare you!"
Mediterranean world. Middle East.

23.13

the fingers of both hands crisscrossed
Pleading. Oath.

23.14

both hands joined before oneself, brought from low to high
Pleading. Exasperation. Italy.

23.15

both hands raised, successively crossed and then uncrossed

Refusal. Negation.

23.16

both hands in front of oneself seeming to wring or twist something

Threat of strangulation.

23.17

the edge of one hand "saws" the edge of the other

Scam, racket.

This gesture, mimicking "sawing wood," signifies that the game is fixed, and that bribes and cheating are involved.

South America.

23.18

both hands joined together as if in prayer, the thumbs and pinky fingers well separated from the other fingers

Stupidity.

The two hands are supposed to represent the head of a donkey. Italy.

23.19

the palm of one hand resting on the back of the other, the thumbs spread wide

Stupidity.

Variant of the previous example, supposed to represent the head of a donkey and its two ears. Italy.

23.20

both hands held out on crossed arms as if to
represent scissors, abruptly separated
The end. Finished. "That's it. There's nothing
left to say."

23.21

the index finger of the left hand planted vertically
in the palm of the right hand, which is held flat
horizontally, the whole forming a T
Gathering. An invitation to join oneself to the
group for a communal event.

23.22

the left hand held flat and planted vertically
in the palm of the right hand, which is held flat
horizontally, the whole forming a T
a. Time is up. Action terminated. A variant
of the previous example, used in certain sports
and in the streets, airports, etc. End of scene.
b. The advertising gesture of Deutsche Telecom.

23.23

both hands together feign to play a flute
Bluster. Uninteresting. "That's a lot of hot air."

23.24

to spread both hands apart and bring them back together several times
Farce; a French practical joke. The definition of the word "compact" mimicking the playing of an accordion.

Hughes Delorme relates that one summer day in Le Havre, he sat down on the terrace of the Frascati by the seaside. The customers at their tables seemed overwhelmed by the heat.

"Now those people there look rather bored," stated Alphonse Allais, "they clearly don't get enough exercise. We shall have to see what we can do about that."

He approached a customer and asked him to define the adjective "compact" with only the use of gestures. The man he had asked then set about a curious exercise. He moved apart his open hands and brought them back together, executing this back and forth motion several times, in order to express the notion of compression. Allais then addressed another customer and asked him to provide the same definition using gestures.

"Let us go," he said, "we will return when they are fully absorbed."

And when Allais and Delorme returned, it was to the sight of all the customers miming the word "compact" and comparing their gestures.

"You see," said Allais, "although the majority of them don't know a single note of music, I still managed to make them all play the accordion!"

23.25

the two hands interlaced and raised skyward, shaken nervously back and forth
Call for help: "Help me, for pity's sake!" This is a gesture of surrender, of entreaty.

23.26

the thumb and index finger of both hands form
a ring, the two interlocked hands form a chain
Human chain. Symbol of trust.
The advertising gesture used by French
banking institution CIC (Crédit Industriel
et Commercial).

23.27

to slide the middle finger of the right hand,
or occasionally the index, into the closed
left fist
Obscene gesture.
Imitation of coitus.
See variants at 26.42 and 26.43.

"... Everything since the Greeks has been predicated wrong.
You can't make it with geometry and geometrical systems of
thinking. It's all this!" He wrapped his finger in his fist.

    Jack Kerouac, *On the Road*

23.28

joining together both thumbs and both index
fingers to form a rectangle
Framing. Viewfinder, aiming.

23.29

the two closed hands before oneself, slightly raised
and lowered to the sides
Imitative gesture. Steering wheel of an
automobile. Children's game.

23.30

the two palms brought together, side by side,
and held at arm's length, forming with the thumbs
and index fingers an isosceles triangle, its point
at the top

a. This gesture evokes the triangle of femininity;
adopted by the feminist movements of the 1960s
and 1970s.

How does one best write the word "cunt"?
   The furious (and rightfully so) ladies of the MLF
[Women's Liberation Movement] drew that word in the sky
during protest days by joining together their open hands.
It's very beautiful. Very Matisse.

   Remo Forlani, *Swear Words*

b. In South America, this gesture refers to
a prostitute.

c. The same gesture can have a Masonic
signification (the Masonic triangle).

23.31

the thumbs and index fingers of both hands touch,
forming an isosceles triangle, its point at the top
Monastic gesture.
The Trinity (for Christian monks), or God in
monotheist religions (on the pediment of
certain cemetery vaults).

23.32

the same gesture, but with the hands held
out horizontally
Bread.
Monastic gesture.

23.33

both hands held out, palms facing down, and lowered slowly several times
Slow down. Gently.

23.34

to loudly beat one's hands together, producing a clapping sound
Applause to demonstrate one's approval.
Airline passengers are often so fearful during flight that after the landing, they applaud the pilot's achievement of correctly landing the plane on the runway.

23.35

to hold both hands cupped together, directing them toward a priest, so as to receive the Host
Communion.

23.36

both hands open, palms up, head inclined
Perplexity. Ignorance. "I have no idea."

23.37

abrupt smack of the palm of one hand against the other, which is closed but not clenched
Obscene gesture. Sodomy.

Brout' made a well with his loosely balled-up left hand, and covered it with the quick smack of the other hand's palm.

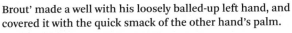

Jacques Jouet, *The Republic of Maïb-Awls*

23.38

to noiselessly strike the fingers of one's right hand
against the palm of one's left hand
Mockery.

His eyes fixed on Broutkowski, Maïb-Awls hit his hands
one against the other, the fingers of the right smacking
against the palm of the left, yet without producing the
slightest sound.

   Jacques Jouet, *The Republic of Maïb-Awls*

23.39

both hands open and thrown into the air,
palms forward
Rejection: "That's enough!"
The gesture made by the Spanish crowds
in Madrid in the days following the bombings
of March 11, 2004, accompanied by the cry
"*¡Basta Ya!*"
This is also the Greek gesture of "*mountza*,"
which is more commonly made with a
single hand.
See 22.38 and 22.39.

23.40

both arms raised, hands spread skyward,
with a slight movement of the wrists
Ignorance. Indifference.

"Do you think people will still be talking about him in fifty
years?"
   "Ah, why, in fifty years? I don't know!" is how you replied.
   I can still see you with your arms raised and your hands
making as if to fly away into the unknown.

   André Beaunier, *In Praise of Frivolity*

23.41

the two hands spread apart, palms facing each other
Gesture that accompanies a look of helplessness, of the inability to answer a question.

23.42

both hands held up, the forearms raised parallel to the body, fists clenched
Gesture of firm determination and strength, carrying with it a threat.

23.43

to wave one's fists
Victory.
Both fists briskly raised into the air in a sign of sporting victory. One can also hold the fist in place, or instead shake it joyously over the head.

23.44

the fingers of both hands interlaced and wriggled in order to caress one's palms
Slight anxiety. Awaiting a favorable outcome.

23.45

to rub the hands together continuously in an enveloping motion

Expectation of an imminent pleasure, relishing in advance a situation that will turn out in one's favor; to rejoice in the defeat of one's adversary.

23.46

the fingers of both hands interlaced and shaken back and forth

Entreaty. The person is leaned forward toward his or her interlocutor in hopes of receiving pardon or forgiveness.

Drawing by Jo Merry
(René Mérigeault).

23.47

to raise one's closed hands, thumbs up at the height of one's hips, imparting upon them a back-and-forth motion accompanied by the same from the pelvis

Obscene gesture.

Simulation of upright coitus.

Love and sex are ... synonymous in the mind of the bovid. Of this part of its being it speaks continuously, with much benevolence and pride. ... The bovid requires a visualization in order to illustrate the virtues of this instrument; and its principal gesture, should it desire to mime said act, consists in raising to shoulder height its hands, closed and overturned, the thumbs turned to the outside. At the same time, its mouth emits a sound indicative of elation. Then, with a curt movement, it seizes in the void two imaginary hips, and savagely brings them back against itself even as its lower abdomen is brought forward and its throat imitates the sound of a motorcycle at ignition. I must draw close attention to the violence of the gesture, which is doubtless quite stylized, for it would be necessary that the hips of the young female be peculiarly supple for them to obey the exuberant movement of our friend, whose hands, in their fervor, are brought far behind him.

Jean Fougère, *The Bovids*

23.48

to trace two small lines in the air on either side of the head, using the index finger of each hand
Parentheses.
This gesture, mostly likely English in origin, is used today by all lecturers.

> I ought to mention that he marked the parenthesis, in the air, with his finger. It seemed to me a very good plan. You know there's no sound to represent it—any more than there is for a question.
>   Suppose you have said to your friend "You are better today," and that you want him to understand that you are asking him a question, what can be simpler than just to make a "?" in the air with your finger? He would understand you in a moment!
>   Lewis Carroll, *Sylvie and Bruno*

23.49

to trace quotation marks in the air on either side of the head by flexing the index and middle fingers of each hand
English quotation marks.
A variant of the previous example.
Gesture of the lecturer.

23.50

to vigorously rub one's hands together as if to wash them
Indifference. Absence of responsibility. "I wash my hands of it."

23.51a

to gradually spread apart one's hands
To get bigger; to put on weight.

23.51b

to bring them together
To shrink; to lose weight.

23.52

both hands open
In Roman antiquity, sculpted on a tomb,
these indicated that the deceased died young.

23.53

*with the thumb and index finger of one hand,
to feign to tear out a hair that has grown in the
palm of the other*
Accusation of laziness. Often used in
conjunction with a French expression, *un
poil dans la main* ("a hair growing from
one's hand"), which is similar in meaning to
Anglophone idiomatic expressions "lazy
bones" or "bone idle."

23.54

to corkscrew the index finger into one's palm
Obscene gesture. Insult. "You know where you
can stick that …"

23.55

*to bring the side of one hand down sharply
against the palm of the other*
Enough. This gesture signifies that one is
cutting short the discussion, often with a
"That's enough!"

23.56

*the fingers of one hand appear to pick something
up from the palm of the other hand*
Money, coins.
This can signify: "He is rich," but can also be a
request for money, a demand.
South America.

23.57

the thumb slid across the palm of the opposite hand
Demand for money. "Pay me!"
The thumb simulates the money that is to be
placed in the hand.
Europe, especially the Netherlands.

23.58

index finger pointed into the palm of the other hand
Disbelief.
"I believe that about as much as I believe in what
I'm holding in my hands."
Middle East.

23.59

to wave one's hands up and down, rubbing together the palms as they pass
Finished.
Satisfaction at having completed an action, at being free of a task that needed to be done.

23.60

to rub the palms of one's hands together, wrapping them around each other
a. Impatience. Looking forward to a pleasant thing (a good meal, for example).
b. This same gesture, in the Middle East, similar to the gesture of wringing one's hands in despair, can express regret.

23.61

standing or kneeling, both palms in the air at shoulder height, the gaze raised skyward
Gesture of prayer and entreaty to the divinity of most religions, especially among the Muslims.

23.62

arms held out at belt height, both palms turned upward
Variant of the previous gesture of prayer and entreaty, which takes the heavens as witness to its veracity.
Middle East, North Africa.

23.63

kneeling, hands placed atop the thighs
Prayer. Meditation.

23.64

the hands held out in front of oneself, palms up
Gesture of entreaty accompanied by an
expressive mimicry.

23.65

the two palms joined together as if in prayer,
head leaned slightly forward, accompanied by the
word "Namaste"
Common greeting in India, Nepal, Thailand ...

23.66

to rub the palms together back and forth
Suggestion of female homosexuality.

23.67

palms laid flat, similar fingers touching, forearms raised skyward

Gesture of prayer in most religions and sects. Entreaty.

Can also simply express asking for forgiveness for a minor mistake or error.

Shandao, wooden sculpture, Japan, eighteenth to early nineteenth century. The Metropolitan Museum of Art, Rogers Fund, 1912. Accession number 12.37.168.

Detail of Jacques-Louis David, *Le Sacre de Napoléon*, 1804.

23.68

to spread both hands apart, palms in the air

Inability to understand a question. Ignorance: "I don't understand, I don't know." Italy.

Belluca had looked at him, a smile on his lips, a look that was almost insolent, his hands open wide.

Pirandello, *The Train Whistled*

23.69
two hands joined together
In ancient Rome, two hands joined together
symbolized harmony and good faith.

23.70
*two hands joined together, holding a caduceus
between two cornucopias*
In ancient Rome, this signified that abundance
came with harmony.

Hans Holbein the Younger.
Printer's device
of Johannes Froben.
Kunstmuseum Basel.

23.71
*both hands held flat and joined at the sides,
opening and closing*
Book. Monastic gesture.

23.72
hands joined together, fingers interlaced
Prayer.

23.73
*to energetically strike the vertical palm of one
hand with the fist of the other, producing a
clapping sound*
Satisfaction. Jubilation. "Yes! That's fantastic!"

23.74

both elbows rested on the table, fists against the cheeks, a pout on the face
Boredom. Impatience.

23.75

both hands held in front of oneself, the forearms turning around one another
Acceleration: "Go faster!" To make haste.

23.76

to raise both hands as if to protect oneself from a danger or a spectacle one does not want to see
Horror. Disgust.
Gesture of eloquence.

23.77

the right hand gives the left a little smack
Self-reprimand.
Gesture signifying that one deserves punishment.

23.78

*both hands lightly cupped and moving as if
they are about to close*
Beckon: "Come here. Come closer."

23.79

*the index fingers of both hands, folded back, are
linked as if they were hooks*
Friendship. Gesture of adolescence.
Variant: with the two pinky fingers.

23.80

*the two palms touch as if for prayer;
bend back the two opposing index fingers;
slide the two hands one onto the other in
such a way that they are inverted;
rhythmically wiggle the two index fingers*
Children's game.

23.81

*bend the index of the left hand back on the palm
while folding the middle finger of the right hand so
as to show its back; place the left hand against the
right hand so that the two phalanges of the left index
finger appear to be those of the right middle finger*
Game of illusion. This is the children's game of
"the severed finger."

23.82

interlace the fingers of both hands with the exception of the index fingers, which remain under the palms; then the index fingers are wriggled

Children's game. In France, *la Cloche*, or "The Bell."

23.83

the left hand holding a daisy, grasping between the thumb and index finger each successive petal and plucking it out

Accompanied by words varying by language: in English, "he/she loves me, he/she loves me not …" In French, *"Il/elle m'aime un peu, beaucoup, passionnément, à la folie, pas du tout"* ("He/She loves me a little, a lot, passionately, madly, not at all"), and so on until the petals of the flower have been completely removed. Divination, fortune telling. Known in English as "She loves me, she loves me not."

23.84

to grasp before oneself in both hands a fistful of chains, throw it back with the right hand over the left shoulder so as to violently strike the back; to again take up the chains in both hands, throwing them back with the left hand over the right shoulder, etc.; each flagellation is accompanied by a half step forward

Mortification, often executed until blood
is drawn.
See also 1.34 and 31.29.
Gesture of the Shiite pilgrims during Ashura,
annual celebration to commemorate the
martyrdom of Husayn, grandson of the Prophet
Muhammad.

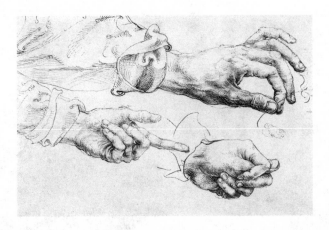

Albrecht Dürer, study of hands.

Michelangelo,
The Creation of Adam.

24

HAND TO HAND

The gestures of the hand are not always solitary.
The hands sometimes touch to share feelings or information,
or simply as play.

24.01

the index finger of the Creator touches that of man,
whom He has created
This gesture—exceedingly uncommon,
it must be said—is perhaps the most
beautiful sharing gesture possible between
two partners.

24.02

to touch the hand of one's interlocutor with one's
index finger while speaking a threat
To punish, "to lay a finger on someone," such
as in the days where the schoolmaster would dole
out "a good smack on the hands" with a ruler.

24.03

to give one's left hand to one's wife instead of the
right hand, during a marriage ceremony
"Left-handed marriage" or "morganatic marriage."
This is the gesture used by a prince or member
of the nobility who agrees to marry a woman of
a lower social rank.

24.04

to hold hands while walking in the street
Friendship, brotherhood, camaraderie.
Gesture of young men in Mediterranean
countries. Little used elsewhere, where it is often
read as a demonstration of homosexuality.

> Here men touch one another
> take one another's hands
> knot their fingers together
> place their palms light as feathers
> on one another's shoulders
>
> Paul Fournel, *You Who Knows the World*

24.05

a raised hand holding a glass
To drink to someone's health.

24.05b

*following the previous gesture, to clink one's glass
against that of one's neighbor*
"To toast" or "to clink glasses" to the health of
one's partner.
Jean-Marie Quitard, in his French *Dictionary of
Proverbs* (1842), cites a maxim that is used when
something is passed around a table from hand
to hand: *A la ronde, mon père en aura*, literally
"All the way around, my father will get his," which
suggests that those who arrived late or are last
to be served will find little to their liking.

24.06

the handshake

The handshake is a sign of confidence, of affinity, of friendship. By holding out one's open hand, one's interlocutor is shown that one is not concealing a weapon. The handshake is not exchanged between men and women as often as between two men. Moreover, not all cultures accept this physical contact. One must not forget among certain peoples the fear of touching the hand of the impure. (In India, for example, tourists are often surprised to see indigenous guides wear gloves; this is simply to defer to the Western habit of touching hands by taking the precaution of not actually touching those of an impure non-Hindu.)

There are many different variations on the handshake. The most impartial is *the presentation of the right palm, turned to the left such that the hand might make even contact with the interlocutor's same hand; after which the fingers close on the hand of the other.* This gesture can be accompanied by an up and down movement, as the hands truly "shake." There are a number of famous handshakes. That between Marshal Petain and Adolf Hitler in the train station of Montoire (in France's Loir-et-Cher region), on October 24, 1940. (This gesture was not anticipated, which is why the photo immortalizing it was not posed.) Equally famous, that between Yitzhak Rabin and Yasser Arafat, standing in front of Bill Clinton, September 13, 1993, in Washington, DC.

Pétain–Hitler handshake,
October 24, 1940.

24.07

One can also *present the palm facing down*, which forces one's interlocutor to *place his hand below one's own*, in a position of inferiority.

24.08

The friendly handshake can be accompanied by other gestures. For example, *to grasp the free arm of one's interlocutor, or even to complete the gesture with an accolade or embrace.*

24.09

One can also *use both hands to envelop those of one's interlocutor*, and then, in some cases, *press on the wrist with one's thumb* (Masonic gesture).

24.10, 24.11

to tickle or scratch the palm of one's partner with a finger

The handshake can conceal another gesture and have an erotic signification (the "tickle" is an invitation, above all among adolescents) or a confidential signification (the Masonic gesture that gave the Freemasons in France the nickname "the brotherhood of the hand-tickle"). Certain rituals can seem excessive to a Westerner:

First you offer them your hand and they grasp it. The clasped hands are slapped then with their spare hand as an affirmation of initial contact. This is, as it were, the soup. Now they pull you to them for the main course, the full embrace, the steak. As you look over their shoulder, your bodies thrust together, your heat intermingled, they crack you on the back at least three times with their open palm. [...] But [these gestures] must be reciprocated. This done, they will let you move away from them, but still holding your right hand.

Hanif Kureishi, *The Rainbow Sign*

24.12

*to gently rub the joints of one's interlocutor's
hand with a back and forth movement of the thumb*
Erotic gesture, if not an obscene gesture of
invitation.

24.13

*to mutually clasp one another's forearm above
the wrist*
Greeting.
This was the gesture of greeting used by men
in ancient Rome. It has begun to see use again,
especially in South America.

24.14

*with arms outstretched, to slap the palm of one's
right hand against that of a friend, a gesture that
may be followed by a striking of the two closed
fists, and, depending on the region, various small
gestures of the fingers, before being completed by
the hooking together of the friends' hands*
This gesture is in contemporary use by young
people, among whom it has completely replaced
the handshake.
This is a gesture borrowed from sporting events.

24.15

to touch the hand of one's partner
"Touching" can signify agreement: buyer and
seller at market touch one another's hand.
This touch is equal to the striking of an
agreement.
This gesture often leads to the following gesture:

24.15b

to "shake on it," which is to say, to vigorously shake
hands with one's interlocutor, palm against palm
Business concluded: it's a deal. "Let's shake on it."
In certain regions, one spits on the ground or
into one's hand before shaking.

"It's a deal!" Illustration by Grévin.

24.16

two people hold each other by the hand
Solidarity.
The chain of solidarity begins with two
individuals. This is the gesture made by
Chancellor Kohl and President Mitterand on
September 22, 1984, before the Ossuary of
Verdun.

Yet no matter how great the losses, our Chancellor and
France's President set an eloquent example, one worth
far more than figures, when they shook hands outside
the ossuary. Because we belonged to the accompanying
delegation—the one that included Ernst Jünger, the
venerable writer and eyewitness of the senseless slaughter—
we saw the statesmen only from behind.

Günter Grass, *My Century*,
trans. Michael Henry Heim, 1999

24.17

the true chain of solidarity begins when three people connect their arms, each person's right hand holding the left of his or her neighbor

24.18

a variant that consists of raising the arms instead of overlapping them

24.19

three hands (from three people) hold each other's wrists to form a triangle
This is more a decorative variant than a true chain of solidarity.

24.20

four hands (from four people) hold each other by the wrist
This is no longer a chain, but a four-handed rescue seat (Boy Scouts, first-aid workers).

24.21

hot hands (or red hands)
Game in which one of the participants, head on the knees of another and hand open behind his or her back, receives slaps on the hand until he or she has guessed the person who slapped it.

24.22

two adversaries, an elbow each on the table that separates them, forearms touching, forcefully clasp each other by the fists, attempting to push down the other's arm, to bend it back until it touches the table

A contest of strength known as "arm wrestling," or in France, *bras de fer* ("iron arm").

24.23

two adversaries hold one another's hand, hooked together by the four fingers but not the thumb; the game consists of pushing down the thumb of one's adversary and holding it on top of his or her fist

Children's game, parody of "arm wrestling" known as "a thumb war" or "thumb wrestling." In French, it is known as *bras de fer chinois*, or "Chinese iron arm."

The game is underway once both players chant a set formula, during which the thumbs touch the accessible points of the adversary's hand.

24.24

to grasp an interlocutor's finger inside one's large sleeve

Negotiation, haggling. A manner of counting in Tibet.

In India, this gesture takes place under a napkin or other cloth.

The Khampas, a people of eastern Tibet, wear ample clothing, the arms of which cover their hands. By shaking hands inside the sleeves, two men can negotiate outside of the view of others by touching their fingers, each of them having its own particular value. This secret gesture is well described in Jean-François Claire's documentary, *In Tibet: The Paths of the Lhasa*, which aired on France 3 on January 17, 2005.

César, *Le Pouce*, Paris, La Défense
(full credit on p. 317).

25

THE THUMB

The thumb is an exception: all of the fingers have three phalanges, the thumb only counts two. But that doesn't bother the thumb, for he is opposable to the other four fingers. This is the tool of the sculptor to which César Baldaccini paid homage by enlarging his own.

This is the first of all fingers: the thumb is the bug-squasher. It is the finger of power, for it is the finger that allows one to hold a scepter or a weapon; because of which it is mutilated as punishment. It's an ancient measurement of length, a twelfth part of the king's foot. The Japanese have a tendency to hide it, as they find it ugly; but they nonetheless use it for counting (it serves as number 5, whereas it is only 1 in Western Europe).

> For the hands have their own quality,
> a world of moving progress
> where the thumb and the pinky
> give the poles of the compass.
> Paul Verlaine, *In Parallels*

25.01

the fist closed, the thumb raised
This gesture has several significations.
a. Satisfaction: OK.
b. Halt: French children often use their thumbs to signal a stop to a game in the schoolyard, or to beg for mercy.
c. Hitchhiking. The raised thumb is the gesture of the hitchhiker asking a vehicle to stop.

d. Direction: the thumb can indicate which way.

e. The number 5 in Japan, the number 1 in the Western world.

f. In Spain and the Basque Country, the raised thumb is the symbol of the Basque separatist movement's struggle. This, for the tourist, is a false friend of which it is good to be aware.

25.02

both thumbs raised at arm's length
Victory.

25.03

the fist closed, the thumb extended downward
This gesture signifies dissatisfaction, disapproval.

This isn't precisely, as it is often said, a gesture from the Roman circus: when there was a desire to spare a gladiator, the thumb was covered by the hand (*pollice compresso*); if, on the contrary, the desire was to see the gladiator put to death, the thumb imitated the gesture of the raised sword that would be brought down (*pollice verso*).

25.04
the hand closed, thumb raised, directed toward the open mouth
Drink.

25.05
to raise the hand and direct it toward the mouth, the thumb and the pinky extended, the other three fingers folded tight to the palm, head tipped back
Drink.
The hand imitates the shape of the *porón* or flask.
Spain. South America.

25.06
to shake one's thumb toward the rear several times
Time has passed. Yesterday, the day before yesterday, last year ...

25.07
the thumb extended and shaken toward the rear
Obscene gesture.
Insult. Homosexual invitation.
Hitchhikers would do best to be aware of this false friend in regions where it is in use.
Middle East. Russia.

25.08

to direct the thumb toward someone in order to designate them

Vulgar and disdainful gesture: "That guy ..."

25.09

to rotate one's extended thumb

Obscene gesture. Insult.

Arab world.

25.10

one hand placed atop the other, the palm of one atop the back of the other, the thumbs rotated like the wings of a bird

Male homosexuality.

The gesture is known as *pajaro* ("bird") in South America.

Not to be confused with 23.19.

25.11

hands interlaced, the thumbs rotated one around the other

Laziness. Idleness: "Spinning one's wheels."

In England, "thumb twiddling" more commonly signifies boredom.

Grandet twirled his thumbs for four hours, absorbed in calculations whose results were on the morrow to astonish Saumur.

Honoré de Balzac, *Eugenie Grandet*,
trans. Katharine P. Wormeley, ca. 1895

25.12

*to gently touch with the thumb the parts of the
body being blessed: the forehead, the eyes,
the nose, the mouth, tracing upon them small
symbols of the Cross*
Unction. Benediction.

... his thumb did not tremble when he dipped it into the
sacred oils as he commenced the unctions on the five parts
of the body where dwell the senses.

    Emile Zola, *The Dream*, trans. Eliza E. Chase, 1888

25.13

*to trace with the thumb the sign of the Cross on
the forehead of the recipient*
Gesture of the priest to confirm the sacrament
of baptism.

25.14

to bite one's own thumb in a menacing fashion
Threat of castration.
There is the tale told by the English traveler
John Evelyn, who, in the port of Genoa in the
eighteenth century, was surprised to see one
boatman address another by putting his finger
in his mouth and biting it.
Italy.

25.15

to suck one's thumb
Obscene gesture.
More an offer of fellatio than a genuine insult.

25.15b

the fist closed, to bring the thumb to the mouth and feign as if to blow into it
Imitative gesture. Trumpet.
Children's game, accompanied by making a trumpet sound with the mouth.

25.16

to bite both of one's thumbs
To regret an action.

> When we do poorly what we must do
> We bite our thumbs, so it is said;
> It is from the sin of the first father
> That this dictum is derived,
> For the gourmand, with his apple,
> Also bit his own thumbs,
> And from father to son, there is why
> The thumb is shorter than its neighbors.
>
> Anonymous, cited by L.-N. Bescherelle
> in *Dictionnaire National*, 1856

25.17

to slide one's thumb between one's index and middle fingers, leaving visible only the small round end of the thumb
Children's game.
It is the adult who feigns to have taken the child's nose: "I've got your nose!"

25.18

inside the closed fist, the thumb is introduced between the index and middle fingers

a. Obscene gesture.

This is the "fig" gesture (in Italy, the *fica*), which compares the vulva to a fruit.

A synonymous gesture is the "olive" of the Pieds-Noirs people of Algeria.

This gesture was described by Rabelais.

> Well then, Mr. Marcel, twas true 'n' certain a false brother! ... If I would have found him an "olive," well, the rabia wouldn't have had to visit him again!
>
> Jean Simonet, *Double Talk*

b. This gesture is also used to protect against the evil eye. It is often presented on amulets (necklaces, bracelets, etc.).

Brazil, Portugal, Southern Italy.

THE THUMB IS
NOT ALONE

As it is opposed to the other fingers of the hand,
it is uncommon for the thumb to be truly alone.
The index and middle fingers are its principal accomplices.

25.19

the thumb, index, and middle fingers extended
and spread apart
Electromagnetism.
This is a mnemonic device that helps one
remember the elements of magnetism.
In French it is known as the *règle des trois doigts*
("the rule of three fingers"); in English it is
called "the left hand rule." In France, the thumb
indicates force, the index finger the intensity,
the middle finger the field.

25.20

the hand raised, the thumb, index, and ring fingers
extended, the other two fingers folded down
Love.
In American Sign Language, this gesture
signifies "I love you."

25.21

the thumb, index, and middle fingers extended and spread apart
The rallying sign of the Serbs of Bosnia Herzegovina (1992) and of those opposing the regime (Belgrade, 1996). Originally, it was a way for the orthodox to affirm their attachment to the Holy Trinity, in opposition to the Muslims.

25.22

the hand held upright, the thumb and index finger open to form the letter L
Initial of the "Laban" ("fight") coalition led by Mrs. Aquino (Philippines, 1986).

25.23

to rub the thumb against the index finger
To ask someone to pay.

25.24

the thumb and the index finger brought together and held horizontally, leaving a short space between them
A little, not very much. "Just a smidgeon."

25.25

the thumb and the index finger pressed against
each other, leaving a horizontal and oval-shaped gap
Obscene gesture. Insult.
This gesture has at its core an imitation of the
female genitalia.
Middle East.

25.26

to abruptly remove the thumb from the closed
hand in which it was contained
Have you got a light?
This gesture imitates the use of a lighter. It
signifies that the smoker is looking for a light.
This brings to mind a bit from Laurel and
Hardy when a flame actually appears on the
thumb and lights a cigar.

25.27

the hand closed, only the thumb and pinky
finger extended
Insult to a cuckolded husband. This is "the sign
of the horns." In eighteenth-century France,
making this gesture could land one before a
tribunal. Alongside it went the habit of saying
"*Honneur à ta femme*," or "Honor to your wife"
(or *soeur* [sister], *mère* [mother]), in order to
show that it was only a joke.

25.28

the thumb and middle finger holding the index finger,
the two other fingers remain folded onto the palm
Argumentation. Presentation of an argument.
A gesture of eloquence used by the orators of
antiquity.

25.29

one's hand held out toward one's interlocutor, thumb extended, index and middle fingers reaching forward, the two other fingers closed
Revolver.
Child's gesture, which is completed by pulling back the thumb as if cocking a weapon.

25.30

thumb and index finger open wide, the three other fingers closed, the hand pivoting on the raised wrist
Ignorance. Incompetence. Impossibility.
Neapolitan gesture.

25.31

to press the thumb against the other fingers of the hand one after another
To pay.
This gesture imitates the pressure exerted on a coin.

25.32

thumb, index, and middle fingers raised, joined together
Blessing.
Not to be confused with certain gestures from Masonic ceremonies.

25.33

the thumb touching the index finger, the other fingers raised, the hand brought near to the mouth
Taste. Excellent, delicious.

25.34

the open hand raised, the thumb and index finger brought together

a. Fragility. Preciosity, affectation.

[Laurent Tailhade] imagines himself to be perpetually holding a rose that he tirelessly offers to everyone, to men the same as women. The "Would you like this rose?" is necessary to explain his gesture—because he carries none—this gesture that astonishes so many people, and with which he rather articulately punctuates so many of his sentences, so pedantically is it drawn in straight lines: the forearm thrown forward in a gracious curve, and, while the ring finger and pinky are closed, the thumb is joined to the index and middle fingers so as to hold the stem of the virtual rose.

L.-G. Mostrailles, *Character Sketches*

b. In Italy, this gesture of affectation can also signify that one desires to know what is going on.

25.35

to form a circle on the horizontal plane with the thumb and index finger joined together at their tips

One of the best-known "false friends."

a. In the United States and England, this signifies "OK," or "Perfect!"

b. In the countries of the Arab world, but also in South America and Germany, this is an obscene gesture that alludes to the anus. This explains why American soldiers were surprised when they were not understood in Iraq.

The same gesture also has other meanings:

c. In Japan, this circle symbolizes a coin. It's a way to request money, but also to haggle over a price.

d. The same circle, in Europe, signifies "Zero," or "That's pointless," which is to say the opposite of the American gesture.

25.36

the thumb and index finger joined together, the three other fingers held aloft
Demonstration.
Gesture of eloquence used by the orators of antiquity.

25.37

thumb and index finger together, the other three fingers closed on the palm
Presentation of a partial syllogism (*enthymeme*), gesture of eloquence used by the orators of antiquity.

25.38

the orator brings together his thumb and middle finger
Exordium. This is the eloquent gesture of the orators of antiquity that accompanied the opening of a speech.

25.39

hand raised, the thumb and index finger forming a circle which is lightly shaken, the other fingers held apart
The circle is the anus, and one denounces, with this gesture, the sodomy of a third individual. Most notably in Turkey.

25.40

the thumb and index barely form a circle by pinching together as if one is holding something between the fingers
Justice.
The fingers seem to hold a Roman steelyard at equilibrium. One signifies in this way that one has conducted oneself in an even-handed manner.

25.41

the thumb and index finger form a ring which is presented vertically
OK. Perfect.
This is a variant to the earlier gesture (25.35), which is ordinarily executed horizontally. It could easily be confused with the next gesture.

25.42

the thumb and index finger form a horizontal ring which is shaken up and down
Obscene gesture. Masturbation.
Very commonly used in England.

Nostradamus.

26

THE INDEX FINGER

The index is the finger of the hand situated closest to the thumb, and it profits from this. By definition, it "indicates." It accompanies speech, for which it is well suited as a substitute: to indicate, to deny or refuse, to assert authority, to insist, even to prophesy, it has no need for words.

In typography, the vignette indicating direction takes the form of a clothed wrist (shirtsleeves and masculine jacket). This drawing today has been replaced by that of a simple arrow, combative symbolism preferred to the anthropomorphism of previous generations. But the index finger has other functions. The French have nicknamed it the *lèche-plat*, quite literally "the plate-licker," which it does quite well. French literature also refers to it as "*le portier de l'Amour*" ("the gatekeeper of Love"), in rivalry with the middle finger.

THE INDEX

The king of the fingers
Which rules over
The hand
The hand
Of the king
Which rules over fate
André Frédérique

26.01

the index finger is extended in one direction,
toward a person or an object
Direction. Indication, designation.
This gesture is the raison d'être of the index
finger: without this gesture, the index would
not exist.
Children understand it well and very naturally
designate people or objects by "pointing with
their finger." However, adults never miss the
opportunity to tell children that "it is impolite
to point."
Is this gesture as natural and as universal as
we believe it to be? It is fitting to remember the
Chinese fable about the disciple who, instead
of looking at the object designated by his master,
looked at the tip of his finger.

Looking very grave, the Prosecutor drew himself up to his
full height and, pointing at me, said in such a tone that I
could have sworn he was genuinely moved: "Gentlemen of
the jury, I would have you note that on the next day after his
mother's funeral this man was visiting the swimming pool,
starting a liaison with a girl, and going to see a comic film.
That is all I wish to say."

Albert Camus, *The Stranger*, trans. Stuart Gilbert, 1946

26.02

index finger raised vertically
Numerous meanings:
a. Authority.
b. Demonstration.
c. Request to speak, for authorization—
to respond to a question, but also, for the
student, to leave to go to the bathroom.

d. A confidence.

e. Bid. During an auction, this is the gesture of the bidder.

f. Triumph. Gesture by which one signifies the number 1, that of the victor.

g. Submission. In ancient Rome, *concurrere ad digitum.* This was to let the battle in the arena continue until one of the two adversaries raised this finger as a sign of submission.

26.03

index finger pointed toward the interlocutor
Designation: "You."
The famous English poster designed by Alfred Leete depicted the face of Lord Kitchener, his pointing finger accompanied by a short slogan calling the young Englishmen to enlist in 1914; this model of the genre was taken up by the United States when James Montgomery Flagg substituted Uncle Sam: "I want you for the US Army." This would be an appropriate time for us to note that poster art often relies heavily on depicted gestures.

Image courtesy of Boston
Public Library
(full credit on p. 318).

26.04

index finger aggressively pointed toward one's interlocutor
Threat.
Gesture that accompanies anger and verbal threats.

26.05

index finger raised aloft toward the sky
Prophecy.
This is the gesture of the prophet, of the
sacred orator.
Sententious and solemn gesture.

26.06

index finger raised and shaken rhythmically
Madness; gaiety.

> It's my hour to swing,
> Yes, my hour to swing,
> Doudadou dadou dadou dadou dadou,
> My index in front I shake,
> As if rattled by a quake,
> And everything is jake!
>
> Georgius, *My Hour to Swing*, 1941

26.07

index finger pointed in a specific direction
Order to execute a specific action.

26.08

index finger pointed at the chest of one's interlocutor
Conversation. Attitude of superiority taken
during the conversation.

Jean-Auguste-Dominique
Ingres, *Oedipus
and the Sphinx*, 1827.

26.09

index finger extended, brought down as if slicing
through the air
Threat.
Germany.

... with his fist clenched and index finger extended he cut
across the air with the menacing gesture of the Germans ...
    Primo Levi, *If This Is a Man*, trans. Stuart Woolf, 1959

26.10

index finger raised, leaned slightly toward the
side of the error
Foul ball.
Refereeing gesture in tennis.

26.11

index finger pointed at the ground
Direction: "Here."

26.12

the right index finger pointed into the palm of
the left hand, as if something were written there
Payment. Request for payment.
Mediterranean world.

26.13

index finger pointed beneath the palm of the
opposite hand
Gathering.
Invitation to get together, to participate in a
common action.

26.14

index finger raised, the other fingers joined with the thumb to form a cylinder
Question: "How are you?" or "How's it going?"
This relatively common gesture calls for the raised thumb in response (25.01a): "OK."

26.15

index finger pointed skyward
Homage.
Collective gesture in homage to a deceased friend. On June 26, 2003, Thierry Henry was joined by the other members of his team in pointing their index fingers at the sky in tribute to their friend, soccer player Marc-Vivien Foé, who died during a match against Colombia.

26.16

to raise one's index finger in the air as one walks along the side of the road, without even turning toward the vehicle arriving from behind
Friendly gesture.
Ireland.

"As the car approached, without turning back, he raised his left hand, his index finger pointed toward the sky. In Naples, it would have been insulting, but here, it's a friendly gesture."

Michel Déon, *Horseman, Pass By!*

26.17

index finger held at arm's length and turned in large horizontal circles
Lift.
This gesture, made on a construction site, is an order to the crane operator to lift the load.

26.18

index finger raised atop a bent arm
Pay attention! Take heed of what the
schoolteacher or superior says.

26.19

*index finger raised, wagged up and down in the
direction of one's interlocutor*
Threat.
This is the warning passed from the
schoolteacher to the student, although it brings
with it little consequence.

26.20

index finger raised, shaken from right to left
Negation. Refusal.

26.21

*index finger held out in front of oneself, making
small circles as if tracing a garland*
Time. Tomorrow.
The more numerous the loops, the further away
in time it can designate.

26.22

*index finger directed toward one's interlocutor,
the finger bent back in a hook as if to draw the
interlocutor closer*
Come closer. Approach. "Come here."

The way we bend the index finger to signal one to
come closer.

   Alfred Jarry, *Days and Nights*

26.23

index finger extended, and then abruptly bent into a vertical hook
Beware, thief!
Japan.

26.24

to draw a circle above empty glasses with one's index finger
Again. Refill the drinks once more: "Another round, please!"

Coussinel tried to catch the eye of the waiter. His finger traced in the air above the empty glasses. A story without words. A full pitcher and two fresh pastis appeared on the table.

  Jean-Louis Viot, *A Good-Looking Dame*

26.25

the index fingers of both hands touch one another and make a slight back-and-forth movement
Disagreement. The two index fingers designate opposing elements.
Spain. South America.
In France, on the other hand, it signifies agreement between two people.

26.26

both hands presented side by side, the index fingers touching and lightly rubbing against one another
Friendship. Those two are friends.
Middle East.

26.27

both hands presented side by side, the index fingers lightly struck against one another
Marriage. They are married.
Southern Italy, Greece.

26.28

both hands presented side by side, the last phalanges of the index fingers struck against one another
a. Obscene gesture. Invitation to intimacy.
Middle East.
b. The same gesture in Japan signifies that it would be best to avoid bringing something up as it might create tension within the group.

26.29

to firmly rub one index finger against the other, both of them directed toward the ground
Dispute. Disagreement.
North America.

26.30

the index finger of the right hand feigns to "saw" at that of the left hand
Insult: Disagreement.
England. Germany.

26.31

the index finger of the right hand passes back and forth across that of the left hand, as if it were being sharpened

a. Threatening gesture among some groups of young people.

b. This is also, among young children, a teasing gesture. "Shame, shame!"

c. Obscene gesture that can signify fellatio: in French, it can mean *tailler une plume* (literally, "to trim or prune a feather").

26.32

the index fingers, slightly bent, connect the two hands as if they were hooks

Marriage.

The fingers are squeezed more or less tightly depending on the solidity of the marriage.

26.33

the two index fingers, bent like hooks, are connected together to form two links of a chain

To carry on. Don't wait, continue, go from one to the next.

Concerts, radio, television.

26.34

the index fingers, hooked together, are conspicuously separated

Ended friendship. Broken union. Rupture.

26.35

to cross one's index fingers, holding them immobile
Cross; crucifix.
Gesture made by monks.

26.36

the extended index finger traces the sign of a cross in the air
Oath.
Italy.

26.37

to touch one index finger in the middle with the other
Half. Midway.

26.38

to briefly bring one's index finger to one's tongue, and then draw in the air the number 1 with the extended index finger
Triumph. One point scored.

26.39

arms raised, both index fingers extended skyward
Triumph. Sporting gesture.

26.40

both index fingers extended in front of each corner of the forehead

Horns.

a. This is the classic gesture to designate a cuckold.

b. This is also the rallying sign of the University of Texas.

26.41

the fist held out, its back presented to one's adversary, the index raised and waved

Obscene gesture.

Threat and insult.

Drawing by d'Escaro for *Le Canard enchaîné*,
September 2001.

26.42

to blow on one's index finger and stick it into the middle of the other hand's fist

Candlestick.

The gesture used by monks to signify fire (blowing on the finger) and the candle (represented by the finger that is stuck into the fist-candlestick).

26.43

same gesture, without blowing

Obscene gesture which monks must not
be aware of (?), symbolizing penetration by
the penis, understood in all countries,
by adolescents as well as by adults.

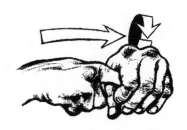

He stuffed the index of his left hand into his closed right
hand and set about some in-and-out.

Roland Topor, *Journal in Time*

(In Shanghai) He sold through gesture: the left index
finger wrapped under the thumb, which the right index,
moistened with saliva, then tried to penetrate.
In Naples, a boy: "Sorella mia" (gestures). "Cinquo
francos" (the hand open before him). "Culo" (index finger
rolled up), "piccolo, piccolo."

Albert Paraz, *The Cattle Gala*

26.44

*the index and middle fingers of the right hand
"straddle" the extended index finger of the left hand*

Insult.
One interlocutor suggests that he could straddle
the other, who would take the role of donkey.
Mediterranean world.

26.45

*to extend the index and middle fingers, waving the
top phalanges*

To smoke. Cigarette. "Got a smoke?"

26.46

to forcefully press and slide the thumb against the middle finger, which then snaps against the palm
Call with insistence.
In Roman antiquity, this is how one summoned the slaves who served at one's table. Today, using this gesture in a restaurant to call the server is considered impolite and arrogant. The student raising his finger should also avoid the use of this gesture toward his teacher.

26.47

to bring to one's lips the gathered tips of the thumb, index, and middle fingers
"Salaam." Simplified greeting in the Arab world.

26.48

thumb, index, and middle fingers gathered and presented in the direction of the person to be blessed, the other fingers folded back
Benediction. Religious gesture. The three fingers signify the Trinity.

26.49

index and middle fingers extended, opened and then closed
a. Scissors (in "Rock, paper, scissors").
b. "Cut."

26.50

index and middle fingers placed vertically on the table, simulating the legs of someone walking
Children's game.

26.51

index and ring fingers extended vertically, simulating the legs of someone walking, while the middle finger is folded back on itself as if the body or head of the character
Children's game.
One can draw the eyes, nose, and mouth of the character on the second phalanx of the middle finger.

26.52

to grasp the index finger of the left hand between the thumb and index finger of the right hand
Argumentation.
Eloquent gesture of the orators of antiquity.
This is also the gesture made by Gabrielle d'Estrées, pinching the breast of one of her sisters.

My father instantly exchanged the attitude he was in, for that in which Socrates is so finely painted by Raphael in his school in Athens; which your connoisseurship knows is so exquisitely imagined, that even the particular manner of the reasoning of Socrates is expressed by it—for he holds the fore-finger of his left hand between the fore-finger and the thumb of his right, and seems as if he was saying to the libertine he is reclaiming—"You grant me this—and this: and this, and this, I don't ask of you—they follow of themselves in course."

Ecole de Fontainebleau,
Portrait of Gabrielle d'Estrées and Duchess of Villars, 1594.

    Laurence Sterne, *The Life and Opinions of Tristram Shandy, Gentleman*

26.53

the index finger of the right hand touches the lower phalanx of the left hand's ring finger
Marriage.
With this gesture, which marks the place one wears a wedding ring, one indicates that the designated person is married.

26.54

index and middle fingers held out in a fork toward the face of one's interlocutor
Threat. Imitates clawing at someone's eyes, without the threat necessarily being genuine.

26.55

to cross the index finger over the middle finger
Protection against the evil eye.
To bring good luck.
One can also secretly cross one's fingers behind one's back.

OFFENBACH: On hearing his name, hold two fingers of the right hand close together, to preserve yourself from the evil eye.

> Gustave Flaubert, *Dictionary of Accepted Ideas*, trans. Jacques Barzun, 1954

Although it took them over an hour to pass by, one might have thought they were only a few squads marching in a circle, because they were all identical, sons of the same bitch, and with the same stolidity they all bore the weight of their packs and canteens, the shame of their rifles with fixed bayonets, and the chancre of blind obedience and a sense of honor. Ursula heard them pass from her bed in the shadows and she made a cross with her fingers.

> Gabriel Garcia Marquez, *One Hundred Years of Solitude*, trans. Gregory Rabassa, 1970

26.56

hand closed, index and pinky fingers extended
Distrust.
The horns. By directing this gesture toward
someone, one sends upon him or her a run of
bad luck or misfortune, a curse. Known
in French as the *scoumoune*, from medieval
argot slang passed through Italian or Corsican,
from the Latin *excommunicare*. This is similar
to the *"mano cornata"* of the Italians, a curse
or the evil eye.
Mediterranean world.

26.57

*index and middle fingers extended behind the head
of the person being mocked*
The horns. But this is not necessarily a reference
to the recipient being a cuckold.

Baphomet also appeared in group photographs when
some joker raised two fingers behind a friend's head in the
V-symbol of horns; certainly few of the pranksters realized
their mocking gesture was in fact advertising their victim's
robust sperm count.
  Dan Brown, *The Da Vinci Code*

26.58

index and middle fingers crossed
Friendship.
These interlaced fingers are a symbol of
friendship: "To be like two fingers of the same
hand." But one can also symbolize the end of
this friendship by uncrossing the fingers.

26.59

*to place the index and middle fingers of one
hand across those of the other hand*
Oath: "I swear it."

Winston Churchill,
June 5, 1943.

26.60

index and middle finger parted to form a V, palm faced forward
Victory.
"Victory will be ours" or "We won!"
This gesture was suggested on January 14, 1941, by a Belgian lawyer, Victor de Lavelaye, as a symbol for the struggle against the Nazis. Adopted by Winston Churchill, this British gesture has since become universal and is used not only by politicians but also by athletes and crowds, including among peoples in whose language the word "Victory" does not begin with the letter V; it is often suggested, in this case, that it designates the Latin word *victoria*, as it was by the Germans, during the Occupation, when they deployed a giant V atop the Eiffel Tower.

26.61

same gesture, but with the palm turned toward the one making it
Obscene gesture. Grave insult.
When he adopted the "V for Victory" (see previous gesture), Winston Churchill knew full well that he ran the risk of his gesture being misread by someone who did not distinguish the orientation of the palm of the hand. This gesture is a very grave insult in English.
While we are quite certain about the precise origins of the previous gesture, the origins of this one are just as uncertain. Some suggest that the two fingers, the index finger and the middle finger, might be those that English archers would use to threaten their adversaries before loosing their arrows.

26.62

same gesture, but the two fingers framing the tip of one's nose

Obscene gesture, Arabic in origin, which is perhaps the origin of the previous example. The two fingers, shaken beneath the nose, make of the latter an erect phallus. (See also 7.34.)

26.63

variants of the V

a. During the Liberation of France, in 1944, the smokers of the liberated population began to use the V gesture, with the index and middle fingers, bringing it to their lips to ask for a cigarette (a gesture observed from Paris to Strasbourg by Jean Nohain, tank officer in the Second Armored Division, France).

b. Vittel mineral water at one point used the V as a gestural slogan. (In cafe bars, clients were to make a V to order a bottle of Vittel.)

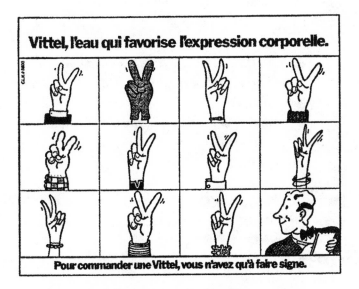

Vittel, l'eau qui favorise l'expression corporelle.

Pour commander une Vittel, vous n'avez qu'à faire signe.

"Vittel, the water that promotes bodily expression. To order a Vittel, all you have to do is give the sign."

26.64

arms raised, index and middle fingers extended skyward in a V
Victory.
Collective sporting gesture.

26.65

index and middle fingers raised in a V
Scout salute. Cub Scouts.

26.66

index, middle, and ring fingers extended in a fork
Scout salute. Three-finger salute used by certain Scout and Girl Guide organizations, and by Scout Patrol Leaders in France.

26.67

index and middle fingers spread and vigorously brandished in the direction of an adversary
Insult.
Simplified version of the Greek "*mountza*" (22.38 and 22.39). Greece.

26.68

the index of the right hand raised, the left hand half-closed to form a well

Parody of a hand game described by Franc-Nohain in a letter to Alphonse Allais (*Le Journal*, April 8, 1894, reprinted under the title "Fragment of a Letter from M. Franc-Nohain" in the collection *Two and Two Make Five*):

Everyone is sitting in a circle, elbow to elbow: each person is holding up their right index finger; the left hand is half-closed, the tip of the thumb grazing the upper extremity of the middle finger in such a way that it forms a small well, an orifice floating in the air. The person leading the game commands, "To each his hole!" or "Community hole!" or "Your neighbor's hole!," and immediately each player puts his or her index finger into the middle of the circle, when the order was community hole, or stuffs it into the little well formed by the neighbor's hand, or into his own little well. You will never be able to imagine anything more entertaining, especially with a little bit of enthusiasm and vigor put into the commands; and I guarantee you that if it happens to be Mme. Marouillet who is calling the game, or even the little Angoulins, to be able to follow them, and, amidst that crisscrossing of hands, to avoid being tangled up in the many different holes, it takes a focus and a dexterity that are quite considerable.

And yet, should one err, it is perhaps even more amusing, for what follows is endless protesting that is exceedingly amusing. "Community hole, Monsieur Burisson; you're doing your neighbor's hole, that's a penalty!—Not at all, to each his hole!—No, community hole!—Your neighbor's hole!"

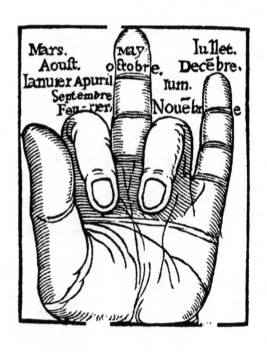

27

THE MIDDLE FINGER

The middle finger is the third and longest of the hand's five fingers. It is also known as the medius (digitus medius), and the French often refer to it as the major (le majeur). Being above the age of majority, the middle finger is for grown-ups.

27.01
middle finger pointed into the air
Approval.
South America.

27.02
Middle finger extended, the other fingers bent down
Obscene gesture.
Insult: "The finger," a.k.a. "the bird." In France, this gesture is known as *le doigt d'honneur*, or "the finger of honor," and thus is the little brother of the "arm of honor" (*bras d'honneur*; see 18.02). This is "to give someone the finger," which suggests doing exactly that (or as the Italians put it, *vaffanculo*). It is one of the oldest of the obscene gestures, used already in ancient Rome, where the middle finger was known as *digitus impudicus*. The emperor Caligula would

offer his middle finger to be kissed instead of his
hand in order to embarrass his subjects.

For indeed he never refrained from filthy conversation and
would make indecent signs with his fingers and would show
no regard for decency even in public gatherings or in the
hearings of the people.

> Aelius Lampridius, *The Life of Heliogabalus*,
> trans. David Magie, 1924

27.03

*the middle finger is extended upward, the thumb
and pinky finger are fully folded down, but the
index and ring fingers are only half folded down*
Obscene gesture.
This gesture begs for tutelage in the correct use
of a pencil! ...
A variant of the "middle finger" in use in Sardinia.

27.04

*with the hand held out horizontally, to raise the
middle finger, holding it perpendicular to the hand,
assisting with the thumb if necessary; the middle
finger is then waved*
Obscene gesture.

27.05

*hand held out horizontally, palm facing down,
fingers stretched out with the exception of
the middle finger, which hangs down, shaken or
wiggled slightly*
Obscene gesture.
Arab world.

27.06

to bend one's forearm up, the middle finger pointed into the air, while the left hand slaps the biceps of the right arm

Obscene gesture.

This brings together the "finger of honor" (*doigt d'honneur*) and the "arm of honor" (*bras d'honneur*), and accordingly is twice as insulting. Mediterranean world.

27.07

the right fist smacks the palm of the left hand, and the middle finger shoots out of the fist at the moment of impact

Obscene gesture.

Very violent gesture.

Middle East.

27.08

to abruptly extend the middle finger, which has been rested on the inside edge of the thumb's last phalanx

Flick of the fingers, snap of the fingers, a negative gesture and gesture of refusal.

"No" as gesture in monastic life.

27.09

the index of either hand raises the extended middle finger of the other hand

Obscene gesture.

Insult.

In Russia, this gesture is known as "Looking under the cat's tail."

27.10

palms brought together, fingers folded back, with the exception of the two middle fingers, which touch together at their tips

Obscene gesture.

This gesture, which forms the feminine triangle, signifies that two bodies have had sexual relations.

South America.

28

THE RING FINGER

*Destined to receive "the ring," the ring finger knows
no specific gestures, unless it is the one spoken of in the legend of
"Carvel's Ring," as immortalized by Rabelais
and La Fontaine. One tradition suggests that a vein in the
ring finger leads directly to the heart.*

Beside her was an onyx bowl. She took from it a perfectly
plain ring of orichalch and slipped it on my left ring-finger.
I saw that she wore one like it.

Pierre Benoit, *Atlantida*,
trans. Mary C. Tongue and Mary Ross, 1920

29

THE LITTLE FINGER
(THE PINKY)

*The little finger is the fifth finger of the hand,
the smallest, and known as the pinky—or in France, as the
cure-oreille ("the ear-cleaner"), because it is small enough
to be introduced into the auditory canal. It is thought of as the
sacred finger, a symbol of knowledge and divination.
It is perhaps the power contained in the pinky that gave rise
to the expression "I've got him wrapped around my little
finger." Raising one's pinky in the air is often considered
a sign of affection and effeminate manners.*

29.01

to extend one's pinky finger in isolation
Skinniness, scrawniness: "He's no bigger than
my little finger."
This gesture may also have an unpleasant and
obscene connotation.

29.02

*to extend one's little finger, then bring it close
to one's ear*
Secret.
Gesture that one makes to a child who is not
telling the truth. The little finger, which knows
all, is supposed to whisper the secret into the
adult's ear.

29.03
raised little finger
Woman.
In Japan, the pinky finger designates a woman,
whereas the thumb, a thicker finger, symbolizes
a man.
This gesture signifies that the woman in
question is a man's companion.
Japan.

29.04
*two people join together their pinky fingers by
bending them into hooks*
Friendship.
Adolescent gesture.
Variant possible with the two index fingers.

29.05
*one person alone can link together his or her own
pinkies as hooks to signify agreement, harmony,
or friendship*
And can signify disagreement or disharmony by
separating them.

29.06
*to raise one's little finger, isolated from the other
fingers, while holding a cup or glass*
Affectation. Preciosity.

THE TORSO

The gestures of the hand surround it and protect it.

Engraving by James Gillray, 1799.

30.01

to sway the torso forward and backward
Movement of the body during prayer or
mediation in many religions.

30.02

to lean the torso forward
The bow. Greeting. Mark of respect.
Rarely takes place anymore in the Western world,
except in certain situations (the maître d'hotel
receiving clients, for instance, or actors bowing
at the end of a performance).
In official ceremonies, men lean whereas women
make something of a curtsey.

Engraving by Gavarni,
Le Diable à Paris, Hetzel, 1845.

This gesture is still customary in Russia, and above all in Japan, where the degree of inclination and its duration depend on strict rules of etiquette.

The room applauded and he seemed convinced that what he was singing was indeed music. Five verses passed by one after another, then he bowed deeply, his left arm dangling, his right hand resting on his chest, then he made his way toward the rear door, turned back, bowed once again, and exited.

J.-K. Huysmans, *A Dish of Spices*

Photo by Kusakabe Kimbei.

30.03

to feign falling backward
Surprise. Astonishment.
Japanese gesture.

30.04

to throw one's torso and arms about
Argumentation.
African manner of starting an argument that also brings to mind the verbal jousting of the Tibetan monks.
Africa.

June 15 [1932]

To keep up the habit, the donkeymen have a dispute lasting an hour or more with a merchant from a caravan we pass going the other way. This man, having lost a donkey and its load, wants to search my donkeymen. They all assemble in front of the leader of my escort, gesticulating, accompanying every point in the argument with a movement of the chest and arm, as if they are throwing stones. Griaule had already drawn my attention to this method of throwing an argument, as one throws dice.

Michel Leiris, *Phantom Africa*,
trans. Brent Hayes Edwards, 2017

31

THE CHEST

31.01
the right hand held flat atop the heart
Pledge of allegiance.
This is also a theatrical gesture used
during presentations.
United States.

Naturalization ceremony,
November 21, 2011.
Photo courtesy National
Archives at Atlanta.

He made a somewhat theatrical gesture, a bit ridiculous: his
right arm traced a large spiral and his hand made its way to
rest over his heart, while he proclaimed with a trumpeting
voice, "I am Alfonso de Albuquerque, Viceroy of the Indies."

    Antonio Tubucchi, *Indian Summer*

31.02
to hold one's hand to one's heart
Love.
This is the typical gesture of a declaration of love.

31.03
the right hand held flat atop the heart
Exhortation for indulgence, appeal to the
generous nature of the person or people
addressed.
Gesture of eloquence that has become common.

31.04

to take the hand of a friend and place it on one's own heart

Love. Gesture that allows the friend to feel the heart beating.

To go along with his mimed sentences, he would always take my hands. One time he took my right hand and placed it on his chest, squeezing it hard: that meant love eternal.

Rosetta Loy, *The Bicycle*, 1974

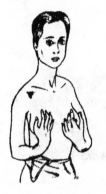

31.05

for a woman to cover her chest with both hands
Modesty.
Oudin (1640) said that in such a circumstance, the common thing to say is, "Is it now Lent that we must hide away the saints and be utterly without beauteous celebration?"

31.06

to clench both hands against the chest, almost at the neck
Anxiety.

31.07

to slide the left hand across the chest under the lapel of one's jacket
Personal gesture often made by Napoleon.

31.08
arms crossed over the chest
Defiance. "You shall not pass."

31.09
arms crossed over the chest
Willingness. Positive attitude.
This gesture can also signify waiting,
with or without impatience.

31.10
arms crossed over the chest
Assertion of authority.
This was a gesture often used by Benito
Mussolini.

31.11
to place one's hand on one's chest,
atop the pocket in which one carries one's wallet
Self-satisfaction.
To make certain, with satisfaction and
ostentation, that one has enough money.

After I defended my dissertation, I resolved to enjoy a few
weeks of rest in a foreign country. You know just as well as I
do the lovely gesture one makes on such an occasion.

You button your jacket with the utmost meticulousness,
then, nonchalantly, you plaster your hand, opened wide, to
your chest in just that spot, in such a way that you can feel
through the fabric the shape and firm consistency of your
wallet. This is the loveliest gesture I have ever made, and I'm
sure the same goes for you.

Louis Codet, *César Capéran*

31.12
*the right hand covers the left hand, which is held
flat atop the heart*
Respect.
Asia.

31.13
both hands crossed and held flat atop the chest
Oath. "I swear it to you."
This is also a gesture used in prayer.

31.14
to hold one's hat flat against one's chest
Remembrance.

31.15
to tap against one's heart with one's right hand
Panic. Request for help.
Common gesture in the Middle East.

31.16
*to touch one's chest with one's fingertips or with
one's pointed index finger*
Identity: "Me."

31.17

the palm of one's right hand placed flat against
one's chest
Questioning: "Who? Me?"
This is also a gesture of denial, for it equally
implies "it wasn't me."

31.18

right hand held flat atop one's heart
Loyalty.
In antiquity, this was the submissive gesture
of the slave awaiting his or her orders.
Remembrance, reverence, during the singing
of the American national anthem.

31.19

right hand on the heart, forearm held horizontally,
elbow at the same height as the hand
Oath.

31.20

to place one's left hand on the heart while the
right hand makes a gesture that indicates distance
and separation
Rather unclear gesture appearing in Eugène
Sue's classic novel, *The Wandering Jew*:

By a movement full of elegance, the girl laid her left hand
on her bosom, and waved her right, which seemed to
indicate that her heart flew towards the place on which
she kept her eyes.

Trans. anon., 1889

31.21

to slide the thumbs along either side of the chest, almost to the armpits, in the place where one's suspenders would lie
Self-satisfaction. See 16.03.

31.22

to strike one's chest with one's fists
Virility. Strength.
One can also aggressively strike one's chest accompanied by a roar to parody the gesture made by Tarzan of the Apes.
Blows to the chest and arms were an expression of pain and mourning in antiquity.

31.23

to shake one's hands up and down, fingers spread, in front of one's chest
Boredom.
Italy.

31.24

the edge of the hand, with its fingers dangling vertically, beats rhythmically against one's chest
Boredom.
This gesture signifies that the interlocutor's conversation is extremely boring.
Italy.

31.25

to simulate the shape of a woman's breasts by cupping both hands in front of one's chest
Physical beauty.
This descriptive gesture expresses a feeling of admiration.

Numerous variants describe the body of a
woman with lesser or greater rudeness.

31.26
*to bring the fingers of the right hand successively
to the heart, the lips, the forehead*
Greeting. "Salaam." Arab world.
During certain encounters, this greeting
signifies: "I give you my heart, the breath of
my soul, and my thoughts." More commonly,
this greeting is reduced to the touching of
the forehead, or the forehead and the chest,
or the mouth and forehead.

31.27
hands crossed over the chest
This is the stance of the child who cannot yet
receive communion; the priest blesses him or
her by touching the forehead.

31.28
parody of the sign of the Cross
Boys' game in France, which might work
somewhat like this in English: the hand is
placed successively on the left of the chest ("The
Cowboy"), on the right of the chest ("The Indian
Chief"), on the forehead ("Have no fear"), closed
fist over one's fly ("You'll get your relief").

31.29
*to violently slap at one's chest above the heart with
the flat of one's right hand*
Mortification. See also 1.34 and 23.84.
Gesture of the Shiite pilgrims during Ashura,
annual celebration to commemorate the
martyrdom of Husayn.

Hyacinthe Rigaud,
portrait of Louis XIV of France.

32

THE HIPS

32.01

fists clenched against one's hips
Anger. Defiance. "He stood there,
his arms akimbo."
A threatening posture.

I put my arms akimbo, and swore like a trooper.
> Anatole France, *The Crime of Sylvestre Bonnard*,
> trans. Lafcadio Hearn, ca. 1890

His anger subsided of its own accord, and, with his two
fists on his hips, he surveyed the assembled guests with a
melancholy and defiant air.
> Gustave Flaubert, *Bouvard and Pécuchet*,
> trans. D. F. Hannigan, ca. 1896

32.02

hands placed on the back of one's hips
Pride. Vanity. Defiance.
A posture of satisfaction.

32.03

for a woman to put a fist against one hip
Gesture of the fashion model intended to
accentuate the bust.

32.04

both hands on the hips
Arrogance.
This is often the stance of the loudmouth
villain in the opera.

32.05

to stuff one's hands into one's pants' pockets
Offhandedness. Disinterest.
Gesture often accompanied by a shrugging
of the shoulders.

32.06

*to turn out the pockets of one's pants to
demonstrate that they are empty*
To be penniless. Poverty (or avarice?).

33

THE WAIST
AND THE STOMACH

It is soft, and it can be fat, even if you tighten your belt.

33.01
to slap one's stomach with the flat of one's hand
Hunger.
Italy.

33.02
to place one's hand on one's stomach and caress it with a circular motion
Hunger.

33.03
both hands (or one hand) flatly patting the belly
Satisfied hunger. "I'm full."

33.04
the fist dug into the stomach with rotations of the wrist
Hunger.
Stomach cramps.

33.05

to sharply strike one's own stomach with one's fist
Japanese suicide.
To feign plunging a sword into one's belly.
"I deserve to die."
In the West, one feigns firing a bullet into
one's temple.

33.06

*with one's fingers extended together, to vigorously
saw at one's belly with the edge of the hand*
Unequivocal refusal.
Nothing, zero. To "draw the line." In France,
this gesture refers explicitly to the belt.

Ludovic, with the edge of his right hand, made as if to cut
across his belly, starting at the left hip and following his belt
across his abdomen to the right hip.

Jacques Jouet, *The Republic of Maïb-Awls*

33.07

*hand resting flat against the belly, accompanied
by leaning the torso forward*
Respect.

When the Persians desired to demonstrate great respect,
they would place their hands upon their stomachs.

G. C. Lichtenberg, *Aphorisms*

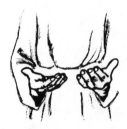

33.08

*both hands held out and flat, palms facing up to
form a platter at waist height*
Communion.
Position for receiving the Host in one's hand.

33.09

*to pull on the front of one's jacket, or with
both hands held flat, to mimic the shape of a
well-rounded belly*
Pregnancy.

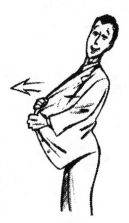

33.10

*the hands make as if to wrap themselves around
a fat belly, the cheeks are inflated*
Girth.
"He's this fat."

33.11

*to give a light (but sometimes painful) jab of the
elbow or fist into the waist of another*
Poke. A friendly nudge.
This can also be a sign of authority or
domination (especially if one replaces the elbow
with the barrel of a rifle).

33.12

to hold one another around the waist
Affection between two people.

33.13

lying flat on one's stomach, arms out to form
a cross perpendicular to the torso, face toward
the ground
Total submission.

This is the position adopted by the priest during his ordinance. In many places of pilgrimage, the faithful literally throw themselves flat on their bellies on the ground, and repeat this bodily gesture as many times as is necessary for them to reach the altar or effigy of the venerated saint. To avoid injuring their hands and knees while violently prostrating themselves, some pilgrims wear thick gloves and kneepads (such as in Tibetan and Nepalese temples).

34

THE BUTTOCKS

*The true foundation upon which both men and women come
to rest. Binary like the cheeks that surround the mouth,
the buttocks are a second face toward which hands tend to stray.*

34.01

to firmly slap someone's buttocks during a game
French game known as *cul salé*, or "salty ass."
This appears around line 155 of Prosper
Blanchemain's enigmatic 1878 poem "La
Friquassée crotestyllonnée," published under
the pseudonym Epiphane Sidredoulx, with
commentary by the author:

Would you like to play a game of salty ass?

Epiphane Sidredoulx's commentary:

"This is one of Gargantua's favorite games. Its name reminds
one of 'Hot Hands' [22.50]. Instead of striking the hand,
one instead slaps the ass of the participant, which will sizzle
away like salt on an open wound."

34.02

*the body leaned forward, to slap one's hand
on the middle of one's rear end*
Obscene gesture.
Threat of sodomy.
Middle East.

34.03

to give oneself a slap on the rear end
Spanking deserved.
"You deserve a spanking," or, "You can cram it up your ass."
Central Europe.

34.04

to give someone a light pat on the rear end
a. Friendly encouragement.
Sporting gesture similar to a tap on the shoulder (American football).
b. This can also be an erotic gesture, especially if the pat is prolonged and includes caressing between the buttocks. The French have an expression to accompany this gesture, *mettre la main au panier*, which literally means "to put one's hand in the basket." A proper spanking, corporal punishment for children, can also be an erotic game between adults.

34.05

to feign wiping one's rear end with a document one has been given
Disdainful contempt that shows how little respect one has for a fine, subpoena, report card, or any other document, official or otherwise, that one refuses to accept or pursue.

34.06

to turn around backward and show one's buttocks
to an interlocutor

Defiance. Insult. Disdain: "My ass!" Also known
as "the full Moon," or "to moon someone."
This gesture is often completed by slapping the
rear end with the flat of one's hand, and even by
sticking out one's tongue.
This can simply be a game that consists, for
example, of showing one's rear end at a window
or some other place where one knows it will be
seen by the most people.

Brout' turned half way around, grabbed himself at the hips
and externalized his posterior, sticking out, somewhat
higher up, a portion of his tongue.

    Jacques Jouet, *The Republic of Maïb-Awls*

34.07

to grab someone by the back of the neck and put
one's index in the cleft of the buttocks while making
him or her run

This is *la course à l'échalote*, a game played by
adolescents in France. It literally means a
"shallot race," perhaps because of the French
rhyme between *échalote* ("shallot") and *culotte*
("underpants").

34.08

to vigorously slap someone's rear end with one's index and middle fingers

Adolescent game.

A painful but friendly game that the French call *la frite*, which Americans would perhaps refer to as "the French fry."

THE GROIN,
THE GENITALS,
THE THIGHS

Fragility, sensitivity, eroticism, they are made to please.

35.01

to place one's hand on the fly of one's pants
Obscene gesture.
Insult. Arab world.

35.02

to place one's hand on the fly of one's pants and raise the thumb
Obscene gesture.
"Here! Smoke it, it's Belgian ..."
This French expression has its roots in the contraband tobacco coming into France from Belgium during the last years of the nineteenth century and the first decades of the twentieth century. This allusion to the fine Belgian tobacco in its package drew a parallel to pubic hair; the suggestion that one smoke it drew a comparison between the virile member and a cigarette.

35.03

to hold out one's hand for a handshake, but, at the very moment one's interlocutor is about to take it, to pull it over to the fly of one's pants and simulate an erection by extending the thumb
Obscene gesture. Adolescent game.

35.04

to slap one's thigh with an open hand, completing the gesture by extending the thumb out from the groin

Obscene gesture.

Gesture used by French cavalry, known as the *basane*.

Among French cavalry, the *basane* was a leather lining that protected the bottom and interior sides of the horseman's pants.

"To peel off a *basane*" mockingly offers up a piece of one's own body, by making the gesture of slapping the thigh next to the groin, "the thumb serving as the pivot and the little finger as the wheeling flank," while saying, "Here you go! For your sister ..." (*Military Cavalry*, 1881).

    Gaston Esnault, *Dictionary of Argot*

> "S'not today you've been made a cuckold;
> N'yet it's just now that you've noticed,
> Ah well, it's happened to Kings,
> An' hey, I'm just having you on ... and here you go!"
> And with that, he peeled me off a *basane*!
>
>   Jehan Rictus, *The Heart of the People*

At which Camus, very calm and still smiling, the astonished Longeverne army behind him, brought his index finger up to his throat and moved it up and down four times between his neck and his chin; then, to complete this already expressive gesture, remembering opportunely that his big brother was an artillery man, he slapped his right hand against his thigh and then turned the hand palm out, thumb against the opening of his fly. "Come and get this, why don't you?" he called. "You dumb cluck!"

    Louis Pergaud, *The War of the Buttons:*
    A Ribald Novel about Boys Written for Adults,
    trans. Stanley and Eleanor Hochman

In a tale by Alphonse Allais called "To Russia, or The Collective *Basane*," an entire regiment offers up a *basane* to their colonel:

Then, without setting down their weapons, two thousand left hands slapped down onto two thousand left thighs, producing two thousand formidable claps.

This gesture was completed with the basane; and what a basane it was, my emperor! And how unforgettable! At the same time, two thousand voices called out together, "Damn! Old fool!"

35.05

to conspicuously place one's hand on one's fly
Self-satisfaction. Pride.

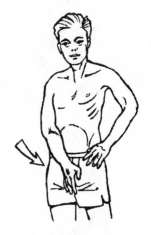

[Jean] Delay is questioning [Jacques] Lacan about a grand reception given at Guitrancourt for the psychoanalysts of his society. Explanation and various anecdotes. And finally: "And then it was also about prestige." And Lacan placed his hand on his zipper with satisfaction.

Raymond Queneau, *Journal*, 1958

35.06

to grab one's testicles through one's pants and give them a shake
Obscene gesture. Insult. Contempt.
Italy.
In Spain, said to signify that the person doesn't like you breaking them.

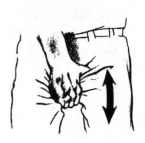

And they even had the nerve to say that the Due Santi, the two saints of the locality ... were ... a pair of "if you follow my meaning," accompanying this assertion with an immodest manucaption-prolation of the pair in question, wrapped though they were in the crotch: immodest, oh yes, but not infrequent then, in popular usage.

Carlo Emilio Gadda, *That Awful Mess on the Via Merulana*, trans. William Weaver, 1965

35.07

to conspicuously scratch one's testicles
Obscene gesture. Defiance. Threat.
"Go fuck yourself!"
Mexico. Southern United States.
In other places, this gesture seems for the most
part to be involuntary.
Regarding this gesture, Oudin (1640) makes note
of this saying:

"You think you're too big for yours," said a man with his
hands in his breeches, giving himself a good scratch.

35.08

to mimic the motion of shaving the hair growing
below one's navel
Boredom. Indifference. "You're taking so long
I'm going to need a shave."
Similar to the gesture of shaving one's beard
in regions where the beard symbolizes wisdom
instead of boredom.
Algeria.

35.09

to scratch one's testicles with the left hand
Conjuration.
Gesture meant to ward off the evil eye.
Similar to "touch wood" or "knock on wood,"
except with testicles.
Italy.

35.10

*to mimic the act of circumcising oneself, the index
and middle fingers imitating scissors*
Racist gestural insult.
Allusion to the circumcision of Jews.

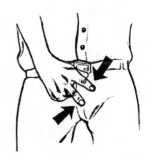

35.11

to repeatedly slap one's own thighs
Stupefaction.
"Now I've seen it all!"
In antiquity, to slap one's thighs indicated that
one was in pain.

Sammy, the new arrival, who had stopped at the rude shout
from his friend, gave himself two vigorous slaps on the
thighs as a sign of his astonishment.

  Pierre Souvestre and Marcel Allain,
  Fantomas: The Hanged Man of London

35.12

*for a gypsy to shake her skirt as if to rid herself
of dust*
Dismissal. "Away with you!"

Le Frou Frou no. 20,
cover illustration by Leonetto Cappiello, 1899.

36

THE KNEES,
THE LEGS

*It was by a hair's breadth that the lower limbs missed
out on being able to make as many gestures as the upper body.
All it would have taken was a wrist.*

36.01

*on one's knees, sitting on one's heels,
the body leaned over toward the ground*
Prayer. Arab world.

36.02

*on one's knees, the body upright,
hands joined together*
Prayer.

In certain pilgrimages, one advances along the ground on
one's knees (Guadeloupe, Mexico), or even climbs a stairway
in this fashion (the Scala Sancta of Sainte-Anne d'Auray, in
the Morbihan department of France).

A certain man was with a courtesan, lying in bed and
enjoying full liberty of the situation, when, at the twenty-
fourth hour, the *Ave Maria* sounded, and the girl sprang out
of bed and knelt down on the floor to say her prayer.

> Michel de Montaigne, *The Journals of Montaigne's Travels*
> (Feb. 1581), trans. W. G. Waters, 1903

36.03

*on one's knees, sitting on one's heels, hands raised,
palms facing up*
Position for prayer. Spiritual elevation.

36.04

on one's knees, sitting on one's heels,
the body leaned down to allow the ground
to be kissed or the forehead to touch
Prayer.

36.05

on one's knees, arms raised skyward
Prayer. Thanks be to Heaven.
Gesture that today is most commonly performed
by sporting victors on the track of the stadium.

36.06

squatting down, elbows pressed against the knees,
hands joined together
Prayer.

36.07

kneeling on the ground, the palms
of both hands turned toward one's face
Affliction, suffering.
Ancient Egypt.

36.08

to bend one knee and place it on the ground
To kneel down on one knee is an infrequently
performed gesture, other than in church at
the altar, or by lovers who still believe in
romantic gestures, and, quite naturally, by
the royal court of England.

36.09

kneeling on one knee,
both arms raised toward a victor or superior
Entreaty. Request for mercy.

36.10

to drag oneself before another,
both knees on the ground
Entreaty.

36.11

to extend one leg behind oneself while both knees
are bent
This gesture demonstrates reverence, an attitude
of respect and deference that has become
rare enough, except for perhaps at the royal
court of England.
The same genuflection, although more emphatic,
is performed by the faithful when they pass
before the sacred altar.

36.12

to slightly raise one knee and scratch it with the right hand
Superstition. To prevent bad luck and ward off the evil eye.
This gesture is recommended if one should encounter three priests at the same time.
South America.

36.13

for a dog, to raise one leg to piss
Gesture observed by ethnographer Michel Leiris, who noted on November 4, 1982:

The dog who invented this bodily technique was a genius: lift the leg ...

37

THE FOOT

They walk the walk.

37.01

to click one's heels together by abruptly bringing the feet together

Respectful salute.

This is the military salute used when one's hands are full; it can be accompanied by a jut of the chin addressed to one's superior. See 13.01. This salute is still found in civilian society in Germany and Austria, where it has lost all military signification.

37.02

to hop up and down or stamp one's feet
Gesture of anger or impatience.

37.03

to tap the ground with one's toes
Impatience. Irritation.

37.04

*to trace a cross on the ground with the tip
of one's shoe*
Insult.
This is "making a cross" on a place that
one curses.
Mediterranean world.

37.05

*to slightly turn one's back to one's interlocutor
and scrape one's feet along the ground as if
squashing something*
Contempt. Boredom.
Italy (Rome).

37.06

to lightly press one's foot, beneath the table,
on the foot of a neighbor
Seduction.
To "play footsies."

37.07

seated or stretched out, to direct the sole of one's
shoe toward one's interlocutor
Very grave insult.
The sole of the shoe being the part of an
individual that treads through the dust and filth
that covers the ground, which is to say all that
is impure, to hold it out to someone is seen as
exceedingly rude.
Middle East and Asia.

37.08

for a motorcyclist in the process of passing another
vehicle to extend the left leg toward a vehicle to
have it get out of the way
The vindictiveness of the motorcyclist can
further be translated into a kick at the body of
the automobile being passed.
Other motorcyclists are usually satisfied with an
arm gesture.
When encountering one another, motorcyclists
greet one another by raising a foot.

When motorcyclists thank you with their foot they
aren't human beings but instead like some species
of earthbound Martian who don't know how to speak
properly with their hands.

Stéphane Sanseverino, *Traffic Jams*

37.09

to kiss someone's foot
Humility.
This is a gesture reserved for one sole
individual: the pope, who, during the Holy
Week, washes and kisses the feet of carefully
selected poor people.

37.10

to spontaneously get to one's feet
Collective gesture of homage.
"The standing ovation": the public stands in
homage to a person (athlete, politician, etc.).
Specialized organizers and presenters have
this gesture be executed with false spontaneity
during television programs filmed before
an audience.

Photo by Martin Thomas
(full credit on p. 318).

37.11

*the spectators in a stadium stand up and sit back
down in turn, starting at one end of a row, which
results in a long wave*
Collective gesture of homage.
This is the *ola* in football, also known as
"the wave" in North America, a very grandiose
gesture, first performed in South America,
and now fashionable on other continents.

37.12

to kick an adversary in the rear end
Aggression.

The kick in the rear end, one of the noblest motions of
occidental anger, is nothing but a vague reflection, nearly
extinguished, of the venerable tradition of impalement.

Léon Bloy, *The Pale*, March 4, 1885

BIBLIOGRAPHY

Bourget, E. *Physiologie du gamin de Paris*. Paris, 1842.

Bulwer, John. *Chirologia, or The Natural Language of the Hand*. London, 1644.

Calbris, Genevieve. *The Semiotics of French Gestures*. Bloomington, 1990.

Calbris, Genevieve, and J. Montredon. *Des gestes et des mots pour le dire*. Paris, 1986.

Drouin-Hans, Anne-Marie. *Le Corps et ses discours*. Paris, 1995.

Edouard, Robert. *Dictionnaire des injures*. Paris, 1967, 2004.

Garnier, François. *Le Langage de l'image au Moyen-Age*, vol. 2, *Grammaire des gestes*. Paris, 1989.

Jorio, Andrea de. *La Mimica degli antichi investigata nel gestire napoletano*. Naples, 1832.

Jousse, Marcel. *Anthropologie du geste*. Paris, 1981.

Lapse, Ivan. *La Langue des langues: Grammaire comparée des langages de gestes*. n.p., n.d.

Mitton, A. "Le langage par gestes." *Nouvelle revue des traditions populaires* 1, no. 2 (1949).

Morris, Desmond. *La Clé des gestes*. Paris, 1978.

Morris, Desmond. *Le Langage des gestes*. Paris, 1997.

Muchembled, Robert. "Pour une histoire des gestes (XVe–XVIIIe siècle)." *Revue d'histoire moderne et contemporaine* 34, no. 1 (1987).

Munari, Bruno. *Supplemento al dizionario italiano*. Milan, 1963.

Picard, Dominique. *Le Corps dans la relation sociale*. Paris, 1993.

Polti, Georges. *Notation des gestes* [The notation of gestures]. Paris, 1893.

Schmitt, Jean-Claude. *La Raison des gestes dans l'Occident médiéval*. Paris, 1990.

Wylie, Laurence. "In Athens, It's Palm-In: Eurogestures Show No Sign of Harmony." *Newsweek*, Nov. 12, 1990.

Wylie, Laurence. "Le Français épinglé." [Interview.] *L'Express*. Aug. 17, 1977.

IMAGE CREDITS

The following are the full credit lines for those figures reprinted in this book under a Creative Commons license.

page 82
Door to the house of Salvator Rosa, Rome. Photo by Paul McCoubrie, available at https://www.flickr.com/photos/paulmccoubrie/7152869721/in/photolist-bZdUDb -bE3HNy-bRHrxa-bEsX1W-dfvEUH-UkWShR-PUSCDP-c2u4Zj-bD7yNQ-bDJSiW -bD7y6d-bTNGya-bU5jXF-bU5jXp-bXxqN9-bU5jY2-pGyu8p (accessed 16 November 2017) under Creative Commons Attribution-NoDerivs 2.0 Generic. Full terms at https://creativecommons.org/licenses/by-nd/2.0/.

page 108
Dizzy Gillespie in concert in Deauville, Normandy, France, July 20, 1991. Photo by Roland Godefroy, available at https://commons.wikimedia.org/wiki/File%3ADizzy_ Gillespie01.JPG (accessed November 16, 2017) under Creative Commons license, terms at https://creativecommons.org/licenses/by/3.0/deed.en.

page 126
Saint Christopher. Line engraving by M. Schongauer. Image courtesy of Wellcome Library, available at https://wellcomecollection.org/works/r4ug39cy under a Creative Commons Attribution 4.0. Full terms at https://creativecommons.org/licenses/by/4.0/.

page 200
Auguste Rodin, *La Cathédrale*, 1908. Photo by Jean-Pierre Dalbéra, available at https://www.flickr.com/photos/dalbera/5506065810 (accessed November 16, 2017) under Creative Commons Attribution 2.0 Generic. Full terms at https://creativecommons.org/licenses/by/2.0/.

page 234
César, *Le Pouce*, Paris, La Défense. Photo by CHAMPARDENNAISAXONAIS available at https://www.flickr.com/photos/26948815@N03/8029562381/in/photolist-dexF2j -dexCs3-dexEAh-dexHQY-dexF1R-dexFYb-dexGDM-dexFo4-dexATL-dexGZH-dexDaQ -dexGjg-dexFoN-dexGF1-dexBgv-dexDhk-dexDJG-dexC3Y- (accessed November 16, 2017) under Creative Commons Attribution-NoDerivs 2.0 Generic. Full terms at https://creativecommons.org/licenses/by-nd/2.0/.

INDEX

forbidden, 17.20
forgiveness, 7.40, 23.11, 23.46, 23.67
fornication, 22.41
framing, 23.28
frankness, 13.18
friendship, 14.11, 15.02, 15.06, 15.07,
  23.79, 24.04, 26.16, 26.26, 26.58,
  29.04, 29.05, 33.11
frustration, 1.14
funny face, 8.39

gaiety, 26.06
gallantry, 8.26, 8.27, 22.105
gathering, 23.21, 26.13
gently, 15.01, 17.29, 23.33
girth, 17.26, 23.51, 33.10
give, to, 22.46
gratitude, 8.31
greeting, 1.32, 4.10, 4.11, 5.01, 7.37, 7.38,
  7.39, 7.40, 8.24, 15.12, 17.03, 22.01,
  22.05, 22.08, 22.22, 22.33, 22.34,
  22.74, 22.75, 23.65, 24.13, 26.47,
  30.02, 31.26
gustatory pleasure, 3.21, 10.10, 10.11

half, 26.37
halt, 17.03, 25.01
hand games, 13.26, 20.18, 22.50, 23.09,
  26.50, 26.51, 26.68, 34.01, 34.04
handshake, 24.06, 24.07, 24.08, 24.09,
  24.10, 24.11, 24.14
harmony, 23.69, 23.70
heat, 22.70
help, 14.06, 31.15
helplessness, 17.14, 18.08, 23.41
hesitation, 1.08, 20.16, 22.19, 22.20,
  23.08
hitchhiking, 25.01
homage, 17.07, 17.45, 20.06, 22.32, 26.15,
  37.10, 37.11
homosexuality, 3.11, 3.12, 5.06, 7.12,
  8.22, 9.01, 10.03, 12.12, 13.19, 14.14,
  20.03, 20.04, 23.66, 25.07, 25.10,
  25.39
horns, 2.10, 3.15, 25.27, 26.40, 26.56,
  26.57
horror, 17.29, 23.76
hot, 8.38
hot hands, 22.50, 24.21, 34.01
humility, 37.09

hunger, 8.02, 8.20, 33.01, 33.02, 33.03,
  33.04

idea, 1.18, 2.06, 4.15, 4.16, 4.17, 4.18
identity, 7.06, 7.07, 31.16
idleness, 25.11
ignorance, 17.19, 22.80, 23.02, 23.03,
  23.36, 23.40, 23.68, 25.30
immaturity, 8.19
imminent pleasure, 23.45
impatience, 20.17, 21.07, 22.53, 22.109,
  23.60, 23.74, 37.02, 37.03
impossibility, 25.30
imprison, to, 20.12
inactivity, 17.28
indecision, 20.16
indication, 13.06, 25.08
indifference, 6.19, 8.18, 10.13, 15.11,
  17.19, 18.07, 22.19, 23.40, 23.50,
  35.08
indignation, 8.04
indulgence, 31.03
inebriated, 7.22, 14.19
innocence, 23.03, 23.50
insatiability, 20.05
insect, 21.09
intelligence, 1.18, 2.02, 2.06, 4.15, 4.16,
  4.17, 4.18, 7.13, 7.18, 7.33
invitation, 14.12
invocation, 17.15
irritation, 20.17, 21.07

jubilation, 23.73

kiss, 8.25, 8.26, 8.27, 8.28, 8.29, 9.09,
  9.10, 9.11, 12.08, 12.13

lack of understanding, 23.08, 23.68
laid-back, 1.27
laying-on of hands, 1.24
laziness, 17.28, 23.53, 25.11
lift, to, 17.18, 26.17
lighter, 25.26
listening, 3.09
look, to, 4.06, 6.13, 6.14, 6.15
love, 25.20, 31.02, 31.04, 31.20
loyalty, 31.18
luck, 1.16, 1.20, 3.13, 11.04, 17.27, 22.73,
  22.103, 26.55, 26.56, 36.12